GILBERTO GIL

musical **/** *trajectories*

GILBERTO GIL

ESSAY
Sergio Cohn

INTERVIEWS
Ana Paula Simonaci
Leonardo Lichote
Paulo Almeida
Sergio Cohn (final edition)

THE INVISIBLE BRIDGE COLLECTIVE

BACKLANDSPRESS oca
andantes LESMOTS MOBILES

Musical Trajectory | Gilberto Gil

SERIES EDITOR AND GRAPHIC DESIGN
Sergio Cohn

TRANSLATION
The Invisible Bridge Collective
Darien Lamen

THE MUSIC TRAJECTORIES SERIES WERE ORIGINALLY CREATED BY
Ana Paula Simonaci | Janaína Marquesini | Leonardo Lichote
Paulo Almeida | Sergio Cohn

PHOTOS
Daryan Dornelles (cover, 14); Personal archive (28, 40, 57, 63, 101); Still from the movie "O Demiurgo",
directed by Jorge Mautner (66); Mario Luiz Thompson (75, 84); Still from the movie "Viva São João",
directed by Andrucha Waddington (92); Paulo Fehlauer (110).

ISBN: 978-989-35445-5-6

THE INVISIBLE BRIDGE COLLECTIVE

OCA EDITORIAL (PORTUGAL, BRAZIL AND ANGOLA)
EDICIONES ANDANTES (SPAIN AND LATIN AMERICA)
LES MOTS MOBILES (FRANCE, BELGIUM AND CANADA)
BACKLANDS PRESS (USA, CANADA, UNITED KINGDOM, SOUTH AFRICA, JAPAN AND AUSTRALIA)

MORE THAN PUBLISHING HOUSES, BRIDGES BETWEEN CULTURES

musical / trajectories

The voices of the world are multiples, just as the ways people perceive themselves. While modern Western culture has predominantly evolved through philosophical and literary contemplation, emphasizing the written word, we cannot disregard the profound influence of music and spoken or sung words, even in these cultures. Music serves not only as a mode of expression but also as a fountainhead of thought. Numerous countries, especially in Africa and Latin America, fundamentally shape their thinking through music, though this phenomenon extends beyond these regions. Over recent decades, music has played a pivotal role in major social changes, firmly establishing itself as a vital instrument for transformation.

Through a blend of biographical essays, interviews, and discographies featuring prominent figures in world music, the Trajetórias Musicais collection offers a flavorful exploration not only into the history of contemporary music but also into significant political and social moments that have reshaped the world.

Published by The Invisible Bridge, a collective of publishers, artists, researchers and translators from different languages and countries – Oca (Portuguese), Andantes (Spanish), Les Mots Mobiles (French) and Backlands Press (English), with the intention of building bridges and dialogues between these cultures, the Trajetórias Musicais collection aspires to be more than just a series of books; it aims to be a political gesture fostering connection and openness to others, promoting candid dialogue, and building relationships between cultures. This endeavor is rooted in the belief that music serves as a vehicle for knowledge, cultural appreciation, and social transformation.

Introduction

From an icon of the Brazilian counterculture to Brazil's Culture Minister, Gilberto Gil has had an exceptionally long and distinguished career. His list of accomplishments includes five Grammy Awards, a discography of over 50 albums, and induction into the Brazilian Academia de Letras, to name a few. But the goal of this extended edition of Music Portraits isn't to list Gil's accolades. Rather, this volume seeks to provide a more personal account of how Gilberto Gil experienced and navigated several seismic shifts in Brazilian politics and culture over the course of his life.

Some of his most poignant reflections on those shifts can be found in his lyrics, liner notes, and past interviews – sources which serve as the basis for Sergio Cohn's biographical essay "Futurible Gil." Cohn's essay presents the reader with richly-textured scenes from Gil's childhood in rural Bahia; his university days in Salvador; and his Tropicalist provocations in São Paulo and Rio de Janeiro – all narrated in fine detail. The broad strokes of Gil's subsequent imprisonment and exile during the Brazilian military dictatorship are widely known. But here again, Cohn's essay draws our attention to the details – an unexpected act of kindness from an army officer; a revelation about macrobiotics in an article about performance art; a deceptive maneuver allowing Gil to perform during the Isle of Wight festival – all of which tell the story of Gil's spiritual self-discovery and musical rebirth.

The idea that an anecdote, an impression, or a refrain can reveal the profound truth of a situation is an approach worthy of Gil himself. This volume includes two original interviews with the artist that shed light on his philosophical and creative commitment to finding large truths in small details. The first explores Gil's compositional process and specific musical influences, while the second takes a more chronological and biographical approach. In both cases, we see a Gil who contemplates conflict and political struggle at a remove (at times to the apparent frustration of his interviewers), while drawing close to the divinity in details.

This focus on details and on the revelation of fundamental truths in everyday life is also the approach of a cultural anthropologist, and it helps to explain the transformative impact Gil had during his term as Culture Minister from 2003 to 2008. This volume revisits Gil's efforts to broaden the definition of culture and to effectively universalize the designation of culture-maker at a particularly crucial juncture in the development of digital production and dissemination technologies. In the second interview, conducted remotely at the height of the COVID-19 pandemic, Gil reflects on the successes and failures of these efforts in the face of a changing digital reality.

We think the stories and details included in this edition of Music Portraits will bring the reader a fuller understanding of Gilberto Gil and his musical thought than all the lists of accolades could hope to do.

Darien Lamen, PhD
Azougue Press, US Editor

Opening act

The best place in the world is here and now. That phrase – sung by Gilberto Gil in the 1977 song "Aqui e agora" (Here and Now) – is perhaps the most profound expression of the philosophy that runs throughout the Bahian musician's life and work. A maxim that condenses Buddha and Bahia; All the Saints of the Baía de Todos os Santos; a deep blue sea that lives in his heart; and the beautiful green of the grassy fields of England.

On the back cover of Gil's first LP, his friend and frequent collaborator Torquato Neto introduced him with the now-famous phrase: "There are several ways to sing and make Brazilian music: Gilberto Gil prefers them all." This condition of "preferring them all" is the opposite of a lack of focus or standards (an empty accusation leveled at Tropicalists like Gil). It is a way of inhabiting the here and now, of embracing the enormity of potential that the present carries – from "beneath the clay of the earth" to the "high, high, highest of dreams" of the Seagull Girl.

Gil enhances the grandiosity of small details while deflating the illusion of man's greatness (in the face of Time, Humanity, Death). Buoyed by the knowledge that it is always here, and always now, Gil is able to maintain serenity in the face of terror (dictatorship, exile, the stupidity of hateful people) because he sees life from the perspective of the gods – from above. He knows and he teaches that "the tartness of the tamarind precedes the sweetness of the mango."

From the "here and now" to "after the year 2000" and beyond, Gilberto Gil has transformed Brazilian song and Brazilian guitar. Moreover, he has transformed Brazil. In his eyes and in his voice, it has become darker and richer, like chocolate and honey. There is no higher or deeper place for a creator than as a popular composer. Part of his life and thought is revealed in the following pages. Let us "loosen the knots in our shoes, our neckties, our desires, and our fears," so that we are ready to take it in.

Leonardo Lichote
Brazilian Journalist and Music Critic

FUTURIBLE GIL

by Sergio Cohn

In Gilberto Gil, distinct forms of human experience come together and coexist, joined by the conjunction "and" ("the most unintelligible word in all of language" according to Fichte): the archaic and the contemporary, science and art, the popular and the erudite, the poetic and the political, the commonplace and the extraordinary, tradition and invention, metaphysics and praxis. All this and much more come together in a trajectory of great integrity and beauty, generating some of the most powerful and innovative expressions of Brazilian culture.

The bringing together of different possibilities, some of them initially opposed, was already a feature of the short-lived Tropicália movement in which Gil was a central figure. Reviving Oswald de Andrade's concept of anthropophagy,[1] Tropicália proposed

1. In 1928, Brazilian modernist poet Oswald de Andrade, invoking the pre-colonial Tupi indigneous practice of cannibalism, famously proposed "cannibalizing" foreign cultural influences as a way of domesticating them within Brazilian creative practices. As he quipped in his Cannibalist Manifesto, "I'm only interested in what isn't mine"

the critical absorption of the foreign instead of an assertion of identitarian purity.[2] This guiding principle is encapsulated in Gil's 1992 song"Parabolicamará," a neologism that unites the communicative capability of the "global village" (the parabolic satellite antenna) and the local term with which Bahian capoeiristas hail one another ("camará" or comrade).

This worldview accompanies Gil through more than five decades of intense participation in Brazilian art and society. It is a worldview characterized by a concern for new technological possibilities, and their impact on our lives. From the electric guitar to the internet, Gil is a pioneer in the use of technological innovations in both the creation and dissemination of his work. In fact, on December 24, 1996, Gil participated in the first livestream of a song over the internet in Brazil. Not by chance, the song was called "Pela Internet" (On the Internet), an allusion to the first recorded samba "Pelo telefone" (On the Telefone), by Donga and Mauro de Almeida in 1916.

Gil's experiences growing up in the Brazilian Northeast were not unlike those of many other songwriters who helped redefine Brazilian popular music in the 1960s – Caetano Veloso, Capinan, and Tom Zé, for example. Their childhoods were spent in small rural towns characterized by a simple and traditional life,

---

2. As visual artist Hélio Oiticica declared, "Purity is a myth." Oiticica created the art installation "Tropicália" (debuted in 1966-7) that gave the Tropicalist movement its name.

while their adolescences were spent in the effervescent "Bahian avant-garde" – Antônio Risério's term for the arts scene in the state capital Salvador during the early 1960s.

Gilberto Passos Gil Moreira was born on June 26, 1942 in Ituaçu, Bahia, where he lived until he was ten years old. As he recalled in an interview with Almir Chediak [1992]:

> *I lived in Ituaçu, a small town with less than a thousand inhabitants at that time. A very emblematic town, the heart of the urban human community. It was a small municipality, but it had a town hall, a tax collector, a post office, city council, judge, lawyer, prosecutor, priest, the parish, the town doctors. There was a public square with a church, with a bandstand, with everything. The town is in the caatinga [arid backlands of Northeast Brazil], but since it's located in a valley on the banks of a river, it is a green, flowering town. I lived there until I was 10 years old.*
>
> *The main references for local music were the accordion player Cinézio, the band Lira Ituaçuense (a philharmonic band), and the guitar players who played at the markets. The markets were on Saturdays. By Thursday or Friday, a few drovers would begin to arrive and generally the guitar players, the singers, came along with them. And the two reference points for recorded music were the music played on the radio, mainly on Rádio Nacional, Rádio Tupi, and eventually on [radio station] Mayrink Veiga – and records, which were very rare too.*

Two or three houses had phonographs or gramophones – in other words, they had a few records. Records by Bob Nelson, Orlando Silva, Luiz Gonzaga. Stuff like that. And, of course, this world opened onto broader musical references. That whole cast of performers from Rádio Nacional, practically all the great successful singers: the Irmãs Batista, Carlos Galhardo, Francisco Alves, Augusto Calheiros, Jararaca e Ratinho, Emilinha Borba, Marlene.

Music has always been a central element of Gil's life. Although he attentively observed the work his father, José Gil, performed at home as a locally-renowned doctor, what Gil really wanted was to be a "musgueiro" – a "musicker." As he explained, the sounds he discovered in his early childhood delighted him [1992]:

The awareness that I was surrounded by music in an enchanted circle – as if some kind of nymph, fairy, or other thing were trying to seduce me – came very early in life. I played with things, I paid attention to nature, to people. I went along selecting things by taste – the good things that were sweet, the good things that were salty, the good sensations in the body, the sensation of being out of breath during the races through the backyard, the fields, the games, the fun – and, of course, I identified with some things and created some affinities.

But with music it was different. Music, when I listened to it, occupied a distinct space within my attention. As if, suddenly, something, someone from a distinct world, was talking to me in a way that other things didn't, in a way that colors didn't speak, densities didn't speak. Music spoke to me directly. It was something seductive, something magical. Early on, at the age of two or three, I'd already decided that, when I could, when I had the ability, I would establish forms of contact with that world. Whenever my mother asked, I would say that I wanted to be a "musgueiro" when I grew up. My father, my grandmother, everyone asked: "What will you be when you grow up?" I'd say: "I'm going to be a musgueiro." I already wanted to make music, to have some relationship with music.

Gil's family was prominent in Ituaçu. His mother, Claudina, was a primary school teacher, and his father, in addition to his work as a doctor, played a major role in local politics. In this way, Gil was able to enjoy a financially secure childhood and also observe aspects of local culture up close that would become important references for him [1992]:

My father was one of two doctors in the entire region. He was a white-haired mulato, *like [the Bahian songwriter] Dorival Caymmi. They were from the same generation and people often mistook him for Dorival on the street. My father went through all the stages of social ascension available to Blacks and* mulatos. *He was one of the, let's say, rare examples of a successful Black petit-bourgeois. I was born in this context. My whole life was structured to carry this forward – to become a doctor, to become lettered, distinguished, to occupy important positions in life – to continue this work of consolidating a Black bourgeoisie in Bahia.*

My father was one of the local leaders, one of the town's political bosses. In part because he was responsible for taking care of a very large swath of the population. Life at that time was politically polarized. My father was part of the PSD and Dr. Luiz Gouveia, who was the other doctor, was part of the UDN.[3] The two strongest parties at the time. Whoever was with the PSD saw my father. Whoever was with the UDN, Dr. Gouveia. It was a really fierce political dispute. Political life was very present in my house and that ended up incorporating local culture. My house was the venue for meetings on religious feast days. When I composed [the 1968 song] "Procissão" [Procession] I'm depicting this experience. The procession used to come right through our door. Another important example was the June [saint's day] festivities[4] where an important segment of the population and the heads of families from the surrounding

3. The PSD (Partido Social Democrata) was a populist political party founded by Brazilian President Getúlio Vargas in 1945 while the UDN (União Democrática Nacional) was a conservative anti-populist party founded the same year

4. The "Festas Juninas" (June Parties) commemorate the feast days of Saint Anthony, Saint Peter, and Saint John. They are widely celebrated throughout the Northeast of Brazil with traditional food, music, fireworks, and bonfires.

farms gathered at our house around a bonfire–my father's grateful patients whom he'd healed.

That's one of the strongest memories I have from Ituaçu. June festivities, religious festivities, civic festivities. The day-to-day of my father's mission-driven life. And the tamarind. There was a huge tamarind tree in front of my house. Every time I see a tamarind, I'm immediately transported there.

At the age of nine, Gil moved to the capital city Salvador to live with his paternal aunt, Margarida, and to continue his schooling. There he began to learn accordion, influenced by Luiz Gonzaga, an accordionist and leading radio singer from the rural Northeast. Gil attended the Regina Accordion Academy for a few years and even formed a band (the Bando Alegre) at his school [2007]:

The first musical phenomenon that made a huge impact on me was Luiz Gonzaga. Largely because of my intimate connection with that type of music.[5] I was raised in the rural backlands of Bahia, in the same kind of culture and environment that provided all the raw material for his work in Northeastern music. Luiz Gonzaga was the first spokesman for the marginalized culture of the Northeast. Before him, the buião [dance rhythm] did not officially exist. It was a rhythm from the remote

5. Gil refers here to the style of music that would become known as "forró."

folklore of the Northeast. Luiz Gonzaga elevated Northeastern music – which until then was just folklore, the stuff of fairs and of troubadours – to a popular culture that was not massified or industrialized, just as João Gilberto[6] did with samba.

Another cool thing about Luiz Gonzaga – and my awareness of this came later when I was pondering the problems of MPB[7] – was the realization that he was also possibly the first big thing in Brazilian mass culture. He was perhaps the first great artist to be linked to mass culture, with his music and performance linked to advertising and promotion. From 1951 to 1952, he signed a fabulous, high-level contract with Colírio Moura-Brasil [Eyedrop Company], which sent him on tours throughout the country.

| 22

In Salvador, Gil moved to the Santo Antônio neighborhood, then an effervescent cultural hub. His life at the time was divided between two realities: on the one hand, he attended an elite school, Nossa Senhora da Vitória, and on the other, he lived in a lower middle class neighborhood which was home to many Afro-Brazilians as well as Arabic and Spanish immigrants. According to Gil [2007],

6. Leading representative and singer of the bossa nova movement.
7. "Música Popular Brasileira," a catch-all term for the Brazilian popular music (above all sung music) that grew out of samba and bossa nova.

I can say with almost total confidence that Santo Antônio was Salvador's most representative neighborhood during that period. It was the neighborhood with the highest concentration of churches, where the Convento do Carmo is located, where the city was founded, where the colonial treaty between the Dutch and the Portuguese was signed codifying the Dutch surrender. The Holy Week procession started there. Nearby there's Pelourinho,[8] a cultural hub that has a very strong significance.

Below, along the shore, there's the port, where there was a big presence of foreign sailors. They would arrive and immediately head for the neighborhood of Santo Antônio. The big Carnival groups, such as Os Corujas (which later became Os Internacionais) and Os Filhos de Gandhi, were all born in the Santo Antônio neighborhood. Santo Antônio was a Black pearl. Today it's in decline, but at that time it was absolutely flourishing. And I was lucky to end up in this place and spend my adolescence there.

Gil had another musical idol at that time besides Luiz Gonzaga, who would remain a strong influence throughout his life [2007]:

When I was a boy, I listened to Jackson do Pandeiro on the radio and thought: "One day I'm going to sing like this guy. I

8. Location of Salvador's colonial slave auction, today a revitalized cultural historic destination.

*have a similar rhythm to him." And he influenced me musically
perhaps even more than Luiz Gonzaga. Jackson's importance
is that he is one of the so-called "cyclical definers" of MPB.
He introduces coco,[9] the northeastern style of malandragem
[cunning and street-smarts], while Luiz Gonzaga brings the
baião,[10] which has its roots in the backlands, in the arid caatinga. Luiz is rural and Jackson is urban. They are, ultimately,
two sides of the same coin, pure expressions of the music from
the Northeast. In my musical training, both are fundamental,
but I'm more like Jackson. I swing just like him.*

In the late 1950s, Gil was part of Os Desafinados, a musical
group composed of friends from the neighborhood, with whom he
played accordion and vibraphone. He was increasingly influenced
by bossa nova, to the point that João Gilberto's guitar-playing led
him to change instrument, adopting the acoustic guitar in place
of the accordion. The impact of that new sound was so great that
Gil still remembers the day he heard it for the first time [2007]:

> *I remember when [bossa nova guitarist and singer] João
> Gilberto appeared. At that time, I was finishing my coursework.*

9. "Samba de coco" is a northeastern variation of Brazilian samba
that often features rapid-fire tongue-twister lyrics and the use of
pandeiro.
10. Baião, or Forró, is a rural Northeastern style of accordion music
that Luiz Gonzaga had helped to codify.

I had already played accordion for about eight years, and I had already enjoyed a thousand forró parties at those rural farms. For me, the accordion was a rational instrument. I had an immediate, mathematical relationship with keyboards. As for the guitar, I used to pick it up from time to time, but I didn't see anything there. I saw six strings and I didn't understand anything – how it was laid out, how it made sounds.

But one day when I was coming back from school, I get home, my aunt Margarida cooks lunch and turns on Rádio Bahia. The song that opens João Gilberto's first LP, "Chega de Saudade" is playing. I said, "What is this?" You know? I had a really strange feeling. I stopped eating, I went and stood by the radio, listening. Then it ended, because João's songs were short.

I spent the entire afternoon studying with the radio on. Then, around 4pm, they played João Gilberto again, this time a different track on the album, but with the same sound. That impressed me terribly. About three days later I met a guy who worked at Rádio Bahia and I asked him, "What was that music that had such a different guitar style?" And he told me it was João Gilberto, a new singer who'd appeared in Rio.

It just so happened that my sister got a guitar for her birthday a few months later. And the guitar remained at home, a strange presence – it was black with a white plastic mouth. And the radio was playing João's music several times a day at that point, so I decided I needed to play the guitar, to do what that man was doing.

That's when I started. I picked up the Canhoto method,[11] I learned the hand positions. As soon as I managed three or four chords that could harmonize the basic songs, I went straight to the bossa nova rhythmic pattern, which gave me a hell of a lot of trouble. Because I only thought of the pattern as a baião, never as a samba. I couldn't relate the samba to what João was doing. I was only able to decipher the pattern with João Gilberto's rhythmic subdivisions when I started thinking about baião. Then it worked. I could only feel the relationship between the bass and the treble strings – that is, the relationship of the thumb and the middle three fingers in the treble – when I started thinking about baião. Nowadays I see that it actually is somewhat related, because João was from up there, from Juazeiro [in the Brazilian Northeast], and there is definitely some baião in that beat. And that's how it was. I kept imitating his soft singing, I tried to play the pattern, I was learning the guitar, playing my sister's guitar for some time, until I asked for a guitar and my mother gave me one.

In the following years, Gil began composing his first songs on the guitar, heavily influenced by bossa nova. In 1962, he performed jingles for advertisements and made his first appearances on television. His composition "Bem Devagar" (Real Slow) was

11. Likely the "Canhoto da Paraíba" guitar method book.

also recorded that year by the vocal group As Três Baianas (which would later become the well-known Quarteto em Cy). Gil played accordion on the recording and the song was released as a 78-rpm single on carnauba wax.

At the same time, Gil began attending business school at the University of Bahia. Those were years of cultural effervescence at the university, thanks to the initiative of the rector, Edgard Santos. He had invited important national and international figures to teach there, including the composers Walter Smetak and Hans-Joachim Koellreutter, as well as Lina Bo Bardi, who was asked to design the Museum of Modern Art in Bahia. However, since the college's campus was scattered throughout the city, Gil did not yet know that students in other areas were also focused on musical creation. Gil only met Caetano Veloso, who attended the School of Philosophy, in 1964. They were introduced by the producer Roberto Santana, as Gil later recalled [2007]:

In 1964, when [Salvador's] Vila Velha Theater was inaugurated, the director of the Companhia Teatro dos Novos, João Augusto Azevedo, decided to put on an Art Week with everything that was happening at the University of Bahia, which at that time wove together high-level art. And he told Roberto Santana to bring together all the people who were making popular music. That's how I met Maria Bethânia and Caetano Veloso. When we started talking about music, they said: "Oh, I know you from television. You like bossa nova."

Gilberto Gil, 1964

I said: "I do, I learned bossa nova because of João Gilberto." Then Caetano said, "João Gilberto! Man, I love João Gilberto." And bam! that whole thing. It was that kind of magical atmosphere. Incredible. Then, in July 1964, for the inauguration of the theater, we did a show called "Nós, Por Exemplo" [Us, For Example]. Caetano came up with the title. It was a show where he came up with everything.

That was my first encounter with artistic production, with this theater-music interface. In this first group – which included Caetano, Bethânia, Gal, Tom Zé – I not only worked as a musician and composer, I also helped with the performance concept. I dove into stage design too, which included a whole world, hitherto unknown: lighting, sets, set design, costumes. My first encounter with these various dimensions and aspects of artistic production took place in Salvador, after the formation of this group. That's when these first encounters happened: the choice of themes, repertoire, song composition. Roberto Santana, who was working in theater then, started to direct.

Caetano was also connected to theater at that time. He'd already developed some music for theater with Álvaro Guimarães, and he was much more into all that than I was. It was João Augusto, Roberto Santana, and Caetano. Bethânia was also very interested in this whole dimension of musical dramaturgy. These ingredients were all present in that first production, Nós, Por Exemplo. Then came other shows, such as Velha Bossa Nova, Nova Bossa Velha, which presented us with new questions – scenographic, musical, practical, etc. It was like training. During that period, from 1964 to 1965 more or less, I had my first encounter with the universe of musical production. It was a collective process, everyone vibrated, according to their affinities. Me, for example, I limited myself more to strictly musical issues, but I was still impacted by all those other dimensions of putting on a show.

In early 1965, Gil was hired by the multinational Gessy-Lever corporation, which was based in the sprawling southeastern city of São Paulo. A few months later Gil moved to the big metropolis, where he began to frequent the city's musical and cultural scenes. He began working as a professional musician, playing on Saturday nights at Bar Bossinha. It was at this time that he also met the playwright Augusto Boal – founder of the Theater of the Oppressed movement and director of São Paulo's Teatro de Arena – who would help Gil and the other young Bahians put on the show *Arena Canta Bahia*. 1965 was also the year Gil met the songwriter and singer Chico Buarque [2007]:

> *I met Chico Buarque in January 1965, when I went to São Paulo to interview with Gessy. When I was leaving Bahia to interview, someone gave me Telma Soares's address. She was a singer and she hung out with a bunch of people who were into music. So in São Paulo I looked her up. And one night we ended up at the João Sebastião Bar, which was owned by Paulo*

Cotrim. It was someone's birthday, and everyone was there. I met Chico that night. We sang, we played. Telma mentioned that I had sung in Bahia. I sang one song, Chico sang another.

We became friends straight away, in a matter of a month or two. At the end of February, Chico visited Bahia with his Architecture program, with his university classmates, and we ran into each other by chance in Salvador. I was leaving work at the Customs Building around midnight – I was a civil servant, an inspector for the Ministry of Finance. I took the civil service exam in 1960, I was appointed in 1962, and I worked there until I decided to move to São Paulo.

Anyway, that night, on my way out of the Customs Building, I ran into Chico in the main square near the Elevador Lacerda with a group of university colleagues, passing the hat so they could buy cachaça. I passed by in a suit and a tie, I saw that group, heard that guitar playing there, and I thought it sounded familiar. I went over and it was Chico Buarque.

In São Paulo, Gilberto Gil's musical career began to take off. He already had some outstanding original songs in his repertoire, such as "Roda" and "Procissão," which were released as a single by RCA Victor in October of 1965. In 1966, Gil first collaborated with the songwriters Capinan and Torquato Neto. Together they wrote the song "Louvação," which became a hit on Elis Regina and Jair Rodrigues' 1966 live album *Dois Na Bossa*. Elis and Jair were the hosts of a television program called *O Fino da Bossa*, where Gil began to make regular appearances. Elis and Gil became friends, and their professional partnership was of great importance to him at that moment. During the 2nd Festival da Música Popular Brasileira on TV Record, Elis performed Gil's song "Ensaio Geral."

In 1967, Gil moved to Rio de Janeiro. He had separated from Belina Moreira, his partner of five years with whom he had two daughters, Nara and Marília. In Rio, Gil began a romantic relationship with the singer Nana Caymmi, daughter of the famous Northeastern songwriter Dorival Caymmi. In May of that year, Gil's first album *Louvação*, produced in Rio by Guilherme Araújo, was released on the Philips label. In addition to the title track, the album features songs such as "Lunik 9," "Ensaio Geral," "Procissão," and "Roda." According to Gil, the album was representative of the type of music that was being made at that time, including a mixture of Northeastern tunes, protest music, samba, carnival march, and baião. The musical transformation that would define his career hadn't happened yet. But his internal unrest was growing.

In February, Gil traveled to Recife to perform at the Teatro Popular do Nordeste. There, he met several musicians and artists who took him to meet the Banda de Pífanos in Caruaru.[12] In an interview for *Bondinho* magazine, in 1972, Gil described the impact of that trip [2007]:

12. A celebrated "fife-and-drum" ensemble that played traditional folkloric music from the Northeast.

I arrived in Recife. I went to do a show at the Teatro Popular do Nordeste. I stayed for a month and the people in Recife were really into this thing of folk culture. At that time, it was very vibrant among university students and whatnot. They had this deep concern for folklore. And since they thought I was one of the composers and artists who was interested in that stuff, they insisted on recording a ciranda[13] for me, and on taking me to see the Banda de Pífanos play in [the rural town of] Caruaru. I wept. I was overwhelmed seeing all that tremendous stuff. So I went back to Rio from Recife knowing that something had to be done in terms of a movement, in terms of integrating those concerns that already existed among the Brazilian students there... where Recife is really exemplary, do you understand?

Back in the Southeast, Gil convened a formal assembly of artists, in the hope of creating a united front of contemporary Brazilian music [2007]:

I came back from Recife and talked a lot with Caetano, Torquato, Capinan, and Rogério Duarte about instigating a bolder and more polemical movement. I thought we ought to shake up the conventional categories. So I had the idea of calling together an Artists' Assembly. We spread the news to everyone.

13. Folk tradition involving call-and-response singing that is performed in a ring.

To start with, we invited the people in Rio de Janeiro: Chico Buarque, Edu Lobo, Sidney Miller, Sérgio Ricardo, Paulinho da Viola. The enthusiasm for my way of thinking was limited to those closest to me: Torquato, Capinan, Caetano. The rest balked. Some for political-ideological reasons. Those who were engaged in the anti-imperialist struggle said that we were pupils of American culture and mass culture. Others [balked] for purely aesthetic reasons, along with a certain dislike of foreign things. The majority of people did have some affinity for jazz and other international musical forms, especially American ones, but they had a lot of difficulty identifying with rock, which was, at that time, what appealed to us the most. For that reason, there was a non-adherence to, if not a deep rejection of the assembly on their part. And in other cases, there was a kind of disinterest and reticence.

Indeed, people were becoming increasingly militant about the popular music of the time, which made it difficult to reach a shared understanding. Proof of this was the "March Against the Electric Guitar" organized by Elis Regina on July 17, 1967. By her side were important figures from Brazilian popular music of the time, such as Geraldo Vandré, Jair Rodrigues, Edu Lobo, and MPB4. While Caetano Veloso and singer Nara Leão watched the whole thing from the balcony of the Hotel Danúbio, startled by what they saw, Gil was in the street, participating in the march.

But as he explained 35 years later, that had more to do with his love for Elis than with ideology [2012]:

> *Caetano didn't want to participate because that [march] had a negative output. It negated a series of things that he was interested in affirming at that moment. In my case, I took myself out of that game. I didn't want to play that game. Had I put those issues at one end of the equation and taken Elis out of the equation, I wouldn't have gone. But I did the opposite. I eliminated all the other terms from the equation and just kept Elis. I took up the position I did for her. The issue was her. I had nothing against the electric guitar.*

The debate around the electric guitar was, as Gil explained, part and parcel of the opposition some MPB artists felt toward including foreign elements within Brazilian culture. The main target against whom those artists were mobilizing was the so-called Jovem Guarda, a made-for-mass-media rock movement starring Brazilian musicians like Roberto and Erasmo Carlos, Vanusa, Wanderléa, and Ronnie Von. These musicians presented a national version of the rock that was emerging worldwide. In the years that followed, they would release some very interesting records, absorbing elements of psychedelic and experimental rock and composing excellent songs. But at the time, their songs were musically simplistic.

By mid 1967, rock music was entering its primetime worldwide.

Artists like Jimi Hendrix, Syd Barrett, Jim Morrison, Janis Joplin, among others, took pop music to previously unknown levels of experimentation. In June of that year, The Beatles released *Sgt. Pepper's Lonely Hearts Club Band*, a definitive milestone, incorporating avant-garde elements and sophisticated arrangements by George Martin. Gil was very aware of all these developments, as he stated at the time in a conversation with the concrete poet Augusto de Campos and Torquato Neto [2007]:[14]

> *I was influenced by The Beatles and by all international pop music. Mainly because they were proposing the exercise of new freedoms within popular music worldwide. And in a blatant way. And because of the lack of loyalty they demonstrated to what had been done before, even in classical, erudite music. The Beatles just about liquidated all the entrenched values of international musical culture that came before. They attempted to put everything on the same level – to put the primitivism of Latin American or African rhythms in relation to the great musical development of a Beethoven,*

14. Here, a small addendum for interested researchers: Augusto de Campos told me that he still has the tape with the recording of this interview, and that it's in his son Cid's possession, alongside anothers tapes with interviews and private performances of important musicians of that time. This would be only the second known recording of Torquato Neto's voice, as well as an important document from the debates of the time.

*for example; to put the recognized value developed in Re-
naissance music, in relation to Scottish folklore, for example.
They take all these things and put them on a single tray, on
a single discursive plane.*

In a debate published by the magazine *Civilização Brasileira* a
year earlier, Caetano Veloso had proposed a "return to the evolutionary line of Brazilian music." Now, in 1967, it was becoming
clear to Gil that the song form needed a more forceful intervention, namely, the incorporation of different musical elements. As
Gil explained [2007]:

> *When Caetano talks about "taking up the evolutionary line
> again," I think we must consider the fact that João Gilberto
> was our first glimpse of a complex formation within Brazilian
> music in which the music was shaped by a series of elements
> that arose not only from Brazilian culture itself, but also from
> international culture. João Gilberto recognized and synthe-
> sized all these things in his work. In [his songs] "Oba-lá-lá"
> – which is actually a bolero, a beguine – and in "Bim Bom,"
> we see the possibility of Brazilian music achieving the kind of
> balance that the new generations of international music ad-
> herents are seeking. This was actually the point of departure
> for João Gilberto. And "picking up where he left off" refers to
> the fact that, after João Gilberto, there was a preoccupation
> with going back to those other very national things – samba*

from the favela, protest music, the "Northeasternization" of Brazilian music, the unrestrained search for themes related to the Northeast, which even culminated in the explicit use of a country "hick" aesthetic, as with [protest singer] Geraldo Vandré, for example. There was a frantic search for things that had been born in our own backyard. So the evolutionary line should be taken up again exactly where João Gilberto left off, in an attempt to incorporate whatever emerges as a new resource within Brazilian popular music, without this concern over what's "international," "foreign," "alien."

All this unrest came to a head during the broadcast of the 1967 Festival da Canção on TV Record, with the seminal performances of "Alegria, Alegria" and "Domingo no Parque" by Caetano Veloso and Gilberto Gil respectively. Their performances united rock elements like the electric guitar with Brazilian music, marking the beginning of the movement that became known as Tropicália. Gilberto Gil's performance featured the revolutionary arrangements of maestro Rogério Duprat, who brought together in the same song the electric rock of Os Mutantes and the berimbau musical bow of Afro-Brazilian capoeira.[15] Gil had initially proposed

15. Duprat became a fundamental figure in developing the characteristic Tropicália sound. He had made a name for himself during the beginning of the 1960s in the Música Nova movement which sought to renew Brazilian classical music.

bringing in Quarteto Novo as his backing band. The ensemble was just starting out and it included the virtuoso musicians Hermeto Pascoal and Airto Moreira. That proved impossible, however, precisely because some of the musicians resisted the use of rock elements, as Gil explained [2007]:

> *I'd gotten the song [Domingo no Parque] accepted into the festival, but I still needed to figure out how to put the arrangement together. I recorded a demo with voice and guitar that I'd already sent in, so now I had to record it properly, with the full arrangement. I initially thought of using Quarteto Novo. They'd performed with [bossa nova songwriter] Edu Lobo on the festival hit "Disparada." The group included Hermeto Pascoal, Heraldo do Monte, Theo and Airto Moreira.*
>
> *I wanted this quartet to do the arrangement with me for "Domingo no Parque," so one day I went to talk with them. Airto and Hermeto were at Canja, which is a music institute that used to exist in São Paulo that was created by the Godoy brothers, from the Zimbo Trio. I said I wanted them to do the performance with me, but with new elements, because I had The Beatles in mind, right? I spoke with Airto, the leader of the group, and I told him I was thinking about a contemporary approach, thinking of George Martin's arrangements. But Airto was very clear, very emphatic, in saying he didn't want anything to do with experimentalism of that sort, that their sound was a Brazilian sound, a Northeastern sound, with a*

Gil and Caetano, 1967

viola [double-coursed ten-string folk guitar]. I was actually a little disappointed, because I really wanted them. I liked them a lot. They were the newest thing in popular music, an ensemble with four heavy-hitters.

So I had to look for another group to accompany me. In the meantime, I commented to Rogério Duprat that I wanted something more Beatles-esque and whatnot, with those elements that fascinated me at that moment, and he said: "Ah! there's a group that works with me on TV Bandeirantes on the Ronnie Von show, and they're perfect for this. I'll talk to them. If they want to do it, it'll be groovy."

The rejection turned out to be fortuitous for Brazilian music: Gil's encounter with Duprat and the Mutantes was seminal for everything that would follow. According to Gil, there was a genuine convergence of interests there [2007]:

Rogério has a position regarding classical music that's very similar to the one we have about popular music – a position of dissatisfaction with the values that have been imposed. He wants to develop classical music; he doesn't want to subject it to an academic sensibility. I think our mutual awareness of one another's motivations is what made our eventual connection inevitable. For example, if you try to figure out how the arrangement for "Domingo no Parque" was done, remember that it was done by both of us at this point where our pro-

gramming was converging. I showed Rogério the music and ideas I already had, and he enriched them with the technical knowledge he commands, but I don't – an understanding of orchestration and instrumentation. But the contours of the arrangement, the decisions about which atmosphere would work for certain parts, which kinds of instruments, which kinds of emotions, all these things were planned together by me and Rogério. In fact, the arrangement was developed little by little. We sat down on consecutive afternoons for four or five days, and we discussed, formulated, and reformulated. And even in the studio, we made additional modifications depending on the sounds that resulted. It was really a job we did together.

| 42

Rogério Duprat agreed [2011]:

The invitation to do the arrangement came from the conductor Júlio Medaglia, who was part of the jury for the [TV] Record festivals. He had envisioned a cinematographic feeling for the song. But it turns out Gil is a well-rounded artist – he always composes very thoroughly – so the arrangement was just for embellishment. As indeed it should be. The arranger is an ornamenter who must work with the art. On the conceptual level, I thought about working with the idea of simplicity and innovation, of originality within redundancy. Along those lines, I followed in the footsteps of [national radio arranger]

Radamés Gnattali, like he did in his introduction of [the samba song] "Aquarela do Brasil."

At every step, I added and I distorted. In fact, there was a convergence of three trajectories: that of Gil, a musician who was well-informed about the Bahian sound; Os Mutantes, the country's first important rock group; and myself, a self-defined cultural guerrilla as well. I combined characteristics of electronic and atonal music – I'd studied with Stockhausen in Germany in the 1960s – with Gil's popular music. By introducing electronic instruments, we made a decision to face whatever criticisms from colleagues may come. Electric guitars were just being introduced into MPB. Established figures such as Chico Buarque and Geraldo Vandré opposed that. They thought it was a form of cultural colonialism. Since I was over 30 years old and had already fought with a lot of Stalinists in my life (having joined the Communist Party at 18), I no longer had the stomach for debate. I just got down to work.

But the fact is that the song was awash in "Tropicalism" generally, which was triggered by the Bahian invasion of São Paulo in 1967. Gilberto Gil was the best musician of them all. Out of the entire hippie group, he was the most versatile. He sang well, played well, thought well. And he was also innovative. He always was, and is, aware of everything. He talks with you and philosophizes. He can see the fly and the direction of flight all at the same time. Constant change is his strong suit, simply because we never know what he's going to do tomorrow.

The highly theatrical and performative element of Tropicalism
was still embryonic in that 1967 festival. But those songs already
contained much of what would become identified with Tropicália, such as the encounter between international pop music
and MPB, as well as aesthetic experimentation that tested the
limits of the song form, costumes incorporating elements of the
counterculture, and innovative set design. Since Tropicália was
not a self-contained movement with a manifesto and clear prop-
ositions, it can be difficult to define. For this very reason, when
Gil was asked what he thought that moment should have been
called, he declared: "'Tropicália' was more exciting, because it
gave an idea of place. It was an ideal situation. 'Tropicalism' was
more like a theory. I found it difficult to understand what it was."

Tropicália's adherents sought to keep all aesthetic options
open for their artistic experiments. But even in the absence of
a clear statement of purpose, their movement soon caught the
attention of many other artists and thinkers. One of the first to
venture some initial impressions on the movement was Augusto
de Campos from Brazil's concrete poetry movement. He immediately understood that there was something new happening
there – something that not only surpassed the limitations of the

Brazilian musical field at the time, but that also introduced a formal restlessness that could solidify into aesthetic innovations. In the wake of Caetano and Gil's 1967 festival performances, he wrote [1975]:

> *It might be said that "Alegria, Alegria" and "Domingo no Parque" represent two complementary sides of the same attitude, the same movement to free national music from the closed system of supposedly "nationalistic" values (which are, in reality, just solipsistic and isolationist) and give national music space for research and experimentation (as in bossa nova's golden days), including in those instances where artistic expression is made for mass consumption (as is the case of popular music) as a way of avoiding stagnation.*
>
> *As with Gilberto Gil's excellent lyrics for "Domingo no Parque," Caetano Veloso's lyrics also have cinematographic characteristics. But, as Décio Pignatari observed, Gil's lyrics are reminiscent of Eisensteinian montages, with their close-ups and their "fusions" ("The ice cream is strawberry – it's red / Oh, the rose spinning – it's red / Oh, spinning, spinning – it's red / Oh, spinning, spinning – Watch out for the knife / Look at the bloody hand – hey José / Juliana on the ground – hey José / Another fallen body – hey José / Your friend João – hey José"). Meanwhile, Caetano Veloso's lyrics are more like "handheld-camera lyrics" in the informal and open way of [Jean-Luc] Godard in that they capture casual reality "in between photos and names."*

Campos's repeated references to cinema are neither offhand nor unusual: Tropicália is an essentially transdisciplinary movement characterized by a convergence of different artistic languages, including that of film. Among the artists who participated were poets (Torquato Neto and Capinan), visual artists (Hélio Oiticica and Rubens Gerchman), playwrights (Zé Celso Martinez Corrêa), filmmakers (Glauber Rocha and Rogério Sganzerla), graphic designers (Rogério Duarte) and writers (José Agrippino de Paula), in addition to musicians like Gil, Caetano, Tom Zé, Gal Costa, Nara Leão, and Os Mutantes. All of them were dynamic figures who created some of the most important works of Brazilian culture. From Hélio Oiticica's installation "Tropicália," which gave the movement its name; to the films *Terra em Transe* by Glauber Rocha and *O Bandido da Luz Vermelha* by Rogério Sganzerla; to the staging of Oswald de Andrade's play *O Rei da Vela* by Zé Celso's Teatro Oficina, the period was replete with masterpieces.

The actual Tropicalist "moment" was short and intense. It lasted less than two years, from Gil and Caetano's performance at the TV Record Festival to their exile from Brazil. During those months, however, the pace of aesthetic research and provocation was frenetic. At the beginning of 1968, Gil released his second album, featuring many "tropicalist" songs such as "Domingo no Parque"; a psychedelic version of "Procissão" accompanied by Os Mutantes; as well as "Marginália II," a quasi-manifesto written in collaboration with Torquato Neto. The album design was developed by Rogério Duarte, an innovative graphic designer and one of the proponents of Tropicália. On the front cover, Gil appears in uniform on a yellow-green background – colors associated with the Brazilian flag and with Brazilian nationalism. On the back, Rogério includes a "psychographed" text by Gil:

> *I've always been naked. At the Regina Accordion Academy, playing [the famous foreign tango] "La Cumparsita," I was naked. All I knew was that I was naked and that next to me was the dressing room, full of colorful clothes – astronaut, pirate, and guerrilla soldier costumes. And me, impoverished in my nakedness, I wanted to wear them all. All of them, so as not to betray my nudity. But they like uniforms. They would accept my nudity, as long as they could then skin me and spread my skin in the middle of the square like a flag or an umbrella. But there is no umbrella against love, against The Beatles, against Os Mutantes. There is no umbrella against Caetano Veloso, Guilherme Araújo, Rogério Duarte, Rogério Duprat, Dirceu, Torquato Neto, Gilberto Gil, against cancer, against nudity. I've always been naked. Wearing the Academy's uniform, I was naked. My x-ray nudity cut through the jeans and striped shirts.[16] And this life isn't easy, so I ask: what clothes should I wear to the samba party you invited me to? What costume are they going to ask me to wear to make my naked body tol-*

16. Another kind of "uniform" also worn by the singer-songwriters of early mainstream MPB (música popular brasileira).

erable? I will walk until it explodes in color. Black is the sum of all colors. Nudity is the sum of all clothes.

At the beginning of the same year, Gil also participated in the collective album *Tropicália ou Panis et Circensis*, a kind of musical manifesto of the movement. The record was produced with Caetano, Os Mutantes, Gal Costa, Nara Leão, Tom Zé, composers Torquato Neto and Capinan, and arranger Rogério Duprat. Gil sings two of his own compositions – "Miserere Nobis," written in collaboration with Capinan, and "Geleia Geral," in collaboration with Torquato Neto. The latter song references the famous phrase of poet Décio Pignatari: "In the Brazilian general jelly [geleia geral], someone has to perform the functions of marrow and bone." According to Gil [2007]:

After "Domingo no Parque" and "Alegria, Alegria," there was an expectation. These songs, and what we'd been doing on TV, indicated a change, a difference. And that was exactly what we wanted. We had to go deeper, to make more songs, and to take more positions. At the time, an album was the most natural way to do that. We needed to make a record with enough substance to suggest what we stood for, what our flag was. And there was interest. Everyone was excited... Guilherme Araújo with Philips, our record company... Tom Zé, Os Mutantes, Rogério Duprat, Capinan, Torquato... The record company, the manager, the artists, the public, everyone wanted it. When someone gestures toward something new, everyone waits to see what the next move will be.

The pressure Gil and others felt to further radicalize their "tropicalist gestures" was accompanied by all the risks of living in an increasingly brutal civilian-military dictatorship. In April 1968, after the "Passeata dos Cem Mil" – a mass demonstration organized in response to the murder of university student Edson Luís – Rogério Duarte was arrested and tortured.[17] In July of the same year, a paramilitary group connected to the government invaded the dressing room of *Roda Viva*, a provocative theater piece by Chico Buarque directed by Zé Celso, and beat up the actors.

The violence was getting closer. But the oppressive climate did not prevent certain acts of courage. During that year's Festival Internacional da Canção, Gil and Caetano performed "Questão de Ordem" and "É Proibido Proibir," songs that were even more radical in both aesthetic and political terms. Gil and Caetano swapped their backing bands from the previous year: Gil invited the Beat Boys, who'd accompanied Caetano on "Alegria, Alegria" the previous year, while Caetano invited Os Mutantes. Gil's performance of "Questão de Ordem" (Question of Order) features the

49 |

17. Duarte later narrated the experience of prison and torture in the book *A Grande Porta do Medo* (The Great Door of Fear), written at the request of Sabiá publishing house in 1968 and unpublished for 35 years, until it was published by Azougue Editorial in the book *Tropicaos* in 2003.

use of microphone feedback and distortion as the backdrop for his clear provocation to the dictatorial regime. Gil's lyrics reference a possible guerrilla war "in the name of love": "You go, I stay / You stay, I go / You go, I stay / You stay, I go / From now on / It's decided / Whoever stays, watches / Whoever leaves, takes their time / Whoever leaves, takes their time / As long as it takes / In the name of love / In the name of love."

The song was disqualified without advancing to the final round of the festival. The jury's bewilderment in the face of Gil's performance, together with the boos Caetano faced during his own performance of "É proibido proibir" (No Prohibiting Allowed), led the latter to interrupt his own performance and deliver a now notorious speech [2008]:

> *Is this the youth who says they want to take power? Do you have the courage to applaud a song this year that you wouldn't have had the courage to applaud last year? These are the same youth who will always, always, kill the old enemy tomorrow who died yesterday! You don't understand anything – nothing, nothing, absolutely nothing! There is no Fernando Pessoa now-adays.[18] I came here today to tell you that the only one who had the courage to take over the structure of the festival – not with the fear Mr. Chico de Assis requested, but with courage – the*

18. A canonical early 20th century poet from Portugal often held up as the "universal" poet of the Portuguese language.

only one who had the courage to take over this structure and make it explode, was Gilberto Gil and me! No one else! It was Gilberto Gil and me!

You're clueless! You don't make any sense. What youth is this? What youth is this? You will never contain anyone. Do you know who you're like? You know who you're like? Is this microphone on? Do you know who you're like? The people who went to Roda Viva and beat up the actors! You're no different from them, you're no different. And speaking of which, long live Cacilda Becker![19] *Long live Cacilda Becker! I'd promised to give this salute here; it has nothing to do with you. The problem is this: you want to police Brazilian music. This year, Maranhão performed a song that was arranged as a Charleston. Do you know which song it was? It was last year's "Gabriela," which he didn't have the courage to perform last year because it was American. But Gil and I have opened a path. What is it that you all want? I came here to end this!*

I want to tell the jury: disqualify me. I want nothing to do with this. Gilberto Gil – Gilberto Gil is with me, so that we can put an end to this festival and all the imbecility that reigns in Brazil. End all of it all at once. We only entered the festival so we could do that, right Gil? We don't pretend. We're not

19. Brazilian actress who headed the State Theater Commission of São Paulo in 1968 and frequently clashed with the Brazilian dictatorship over censorship.

pretending that we don't know what festivals are all about, no. Nobody ever heard me talk like that. Got it? That's all I wanted to say, baby. You know how it is? We – he and I – had the courage to enter all the structures and then leave them all. And you? If you are... If you, in politics, are the way you are in aesthetics, we're done! Disqualify me along with Gil! Along with him, do you understand? And as for you... The jury is very nice, but it's incompetent. God is on the loose! Out of tune, no melody? What's that, jury? You didn't get it right? You rated Gilberto Gil's melody? You missed out. Gil blew your minds, huh? That's what I want to see. Enough!

Gil recalled the impact of that scene [2007]:

Well, I was there in the audience, watching "É Proibido Proibir," Caetano with Os Mutantes. Caetano interrupted the performance and started the speech and I went up to the stage. He said, "Gil is here, Gil is with me." And the angry mob was throwing things. I remember a piece of the set hit my shin. And I was there in the middle of everything, feeling that heat of public performance I've felt since I was 10... I was scared. But at the same time, standing on that stage next to Caetano, I had a certain ironic smile in my heart, as if to say: this actually turned out the way it needed to. They didn't understand that we didn't want a confrontation, that our aim was to bring an ever greater number of people to enjoy new ways of creating.

I knew, hence my wry smile. Almost two years earlier, in 1967, the Assembly we called for in Rio had already shown me that – creative people, people with Rio de Janeiro's degree of intelligence, had already had that same conventional reaction of an audience that is opposed to anything challenging.

The Tropicalists' insistence on aesthetic and individual revolution was not able to ward off the dark cloud that gathered over the country. In August 1968, another Tropicalist event was marred by tragedy. The idea had been to do a show at the Gafieira Som de Cristal nightclub with special guests that included singer Vicente Celestino. Caetano had re-recorded Celestino's song "Coração Materno" for a recent album, helping to revive interest in the older man's music long after he had been written off as corny and unsophisticated. Celestino, who was already more than 70 years old at the time, was pleased with the tribute. But something he saw on the day of the show left him shaken. According to Gil [2007]:

Zé Celso was directing the pilot for what was supposed to be a TV series. It was supposed to be a summation of Tropicália in all its dimensions. I think I was going to sing "Geleia Geral." I don't remember. The set design Zé Celso came up with was the Last Supper, with the apostles' table and a basket of tropical fruits instead of bread. Me, with a mustache, goatee, and long hair – I was Christ. I had to sing and host the program from the center of the table, dressed in a cape and some quintessentially Tropicália clothes. Vicente Celestino, Dircinha Batista, and Dalva de Oliveira were some of the guests.

In the afternoon, during the rehearsal, Vicente was in the audience. When I finished the rehearsal, he stood up and snarled something like: "A Black Christ I can live with, but bananas in place of bread is disrespectful." And this was coming from a gentleman, an icon, the symbol of an era, right? And from our invited guest, [since] Caetano had recorded [Celestino's song] "Coração Materno." I was really devastated by Vicente's reaction, as if he had caught us committing some disrespectful act. And once again, along came that conflict between the aesthetic dream and the reality of things. I wasn't there to fight, I was there for the art. I've always had a hard time being a politician. I left deeply depressed and dispirited.

That was in the afternoon. When we returned home, I told Caetano I didn't want to do the program, that I didn't have the energy to set foot on stage. Caetano said my fear was unacceptable. About an hour later we got word at home that Vicente Celestino had died of a heart attack at the Hotel Normandie. That night, I did the show in a daze. Aside from my time in prison, I think that was the most harrowing day of my life. Vicente had told Caetano he didn't want to do the program and he died. He was the harbinger for the vague threat that was looming over us.

In December of that year, the threat materialized. On December 13th, the government enacted Institutional Act 5 (AI-5), which marked the beginning of the dictatorship's most violent phase. Two days after Christmas, Gil and Caetano were arrested in São Paulo and taken in a police vehicle to Rio de Janeiro. There, they were held in solitary confinement for a week. Gil later said he couldn't recall "having lived a sadder week." From there, they were sent to the Vila Militar in Rio, where Gil was kept in a larger cell with other political prisoners, including artists and writers such as Ferreira Gullar, a teenage Perfeito Fortuna, and Antônio Callado. Caetano was held in a building next door. From there they were taken to the Paratrooper Regiment in nearby Deodoro, where Gil was again placed in an individual cell.

In Deodoro, Gil was interrogated by the military and given a guitar by a Sergeant Juarez (whose name Gil would never forget). With the guitar, Gil composed several songs that became part of his next album, including "Futurível" (Futurible), "Vitrines" (Display Windows), and "Cérebro Eletrônico" (Electronic Brain). It was in prison that Gil also decided to adopt a macrobiotic diet and to pursue his interest in Eastern philosophy. On February 25, 1969, after two months in detention and without any formal charges filed, a police escort took Caetano and Gil to Salvador in a Brazilian Air Force plane. There they were released under military custody. They remained in this situation for a few more months, unable to work, make public appearances, or give interviews, until they received a proposal to leave the country in exile. As

Gil explained, the colonel responsible for their custody was the one who broached the idea [2007]:

> *Colonel Luiz Arthur, who was in charge of our custody, spent the first two, three months simply carrying out the Army's orders. Later on, he started to question why he wasn't forwarded any investigation or formal charges, nothing that would give him the legal instruments to keep us in custody. He began to question all of this, and so this colonel began to stick his neck out.*
>
> *He was the one who negotiated our exit from Brazil, challenging precisely the lack of investigation or charges. He went to Rio and returned with the following position: "The Army – in short, the dictatorship, the central power – indicated there's a possibility for you to leave Brazil." We asked questions, we analyzed, and we ended up considering this possibility.*
>
> *And so then comes the problem of how to make this work, and, first of all, how to make our situation known, how to give some kind of explanation to the public. We also wanted some minimal compensation out of the whole thing. The situation was being negotiated, this was clear. So we negotiated the recording of an album with the possibility of some interviews. I would make a record, Caetano would make another. All in Bahia, in Salvador. Rogério Duprat would go there, get the recorded material, and bring it to Rio and São Paulo to add to it. In addition, we negotiated a farewell concert which,*

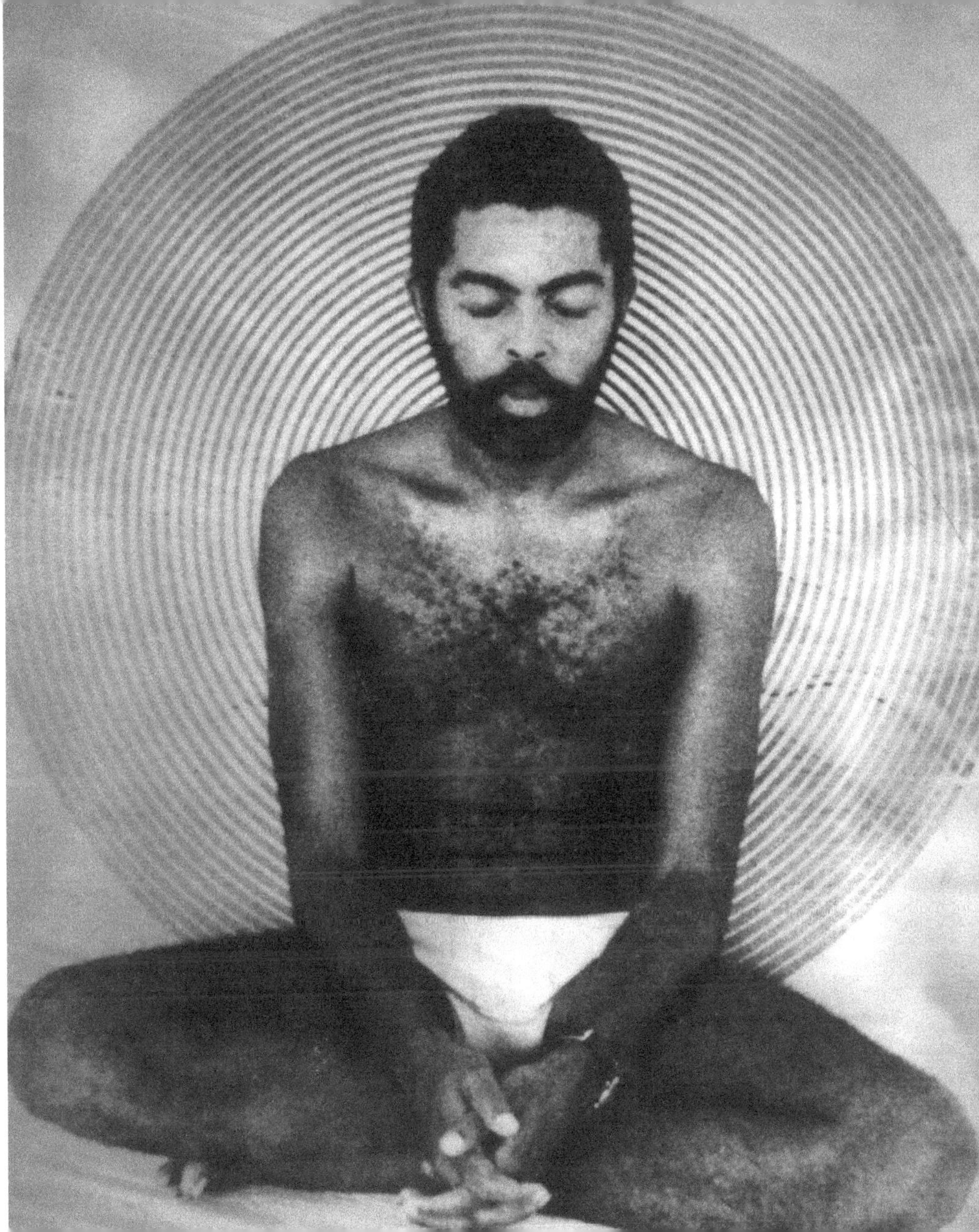

Gil's third album, recorded under duress in this way, was one of the most interesting of his career, with compositions that deal with science fiction themes, such as space travel and cybernetic advances, including the three aforementioned songs written in prison. In addition, the splendid track "Objeto Semi-Identificado," by Gil and Rogério Duarte, features considerable formal experimentation, with lyrics recited by the two composers and sound collages made by Rogério Duprat.

In a strange way, Gil and Caetano's farewell albums would only serve to consolidate Tropicália's musical influence. With the exile of its two main agitators, the movement was interrupted. But according to Gil, this premature end was key to the importance Tropicália came to assume in Brazilian culture [2007]:

> Tropicalism's abrupt interruption is what consolidated
> the rupture it had wanted to make in Brazilian music and
> art. If the movement hadn't been recognized as an abuse, or
> confused with abuse, it wouldn't have been recognized as a
> new exuberant use of every potential. Even if much of what

it generated had remained and given way to other things, it wouldn't be the historic watershed that it is. It wouldn't provoke analytical curiosity.

Tropicalism was a short period during which we were contested leaders. Then it became a cult. The legacy of Tropicalism was that Brazilian culture assimilated experimentalism – the moderate experimentalism that was possible within the culture industry. But it was our efforts post-Tropicalism that made the movement an object of respect.

According to Gil, Tropicália was more important as a cultural movement than a strictly musical one. Fifty years later, he stated [2018]:

I often say, somewhat irresponsibly, that Tropicalism was not, strictly speaking, a musical movement, with essentially musical transformations, like bossa nova was. And I usually go even further: that this happened because of a deficiency we had, a technical deficit. We didn't have a proficient command of certain instruments, like Tom Jobim had with the piano, or like João Gilberto had with the guitar. We were rustic in this sense, we were beginner musicians who hadn't yet mastered the language fully. And for this reason and many others, I usually say that Tropicalism didn't cause a properly musical revolution, like bossa nova and Jovem Guarda. Jovem Guarda created a language with electric guitars, absorbing elements from the world of light song and rock, just as bossa nova had done from the world of samba and jazz.

In exile, Gil quickly passed through Portugal and France before settling in London, England, for about three years. There, he immersed himself in the counterculture and in what remained of 1960s Swinging London, taking hallucinogens, living in collective housing, and attending concerts by the big names of the time. It was an important period in Gil's musical education. It was the moment he pushed himself to overcome the technical deficit he identified in the Tropicalist period [2007]:

> *In Brazil, I was a songmaker who happened to play the guitar. I didn't have an opportunity to delve into the instrument. When I arrived in England, I was startled by the level, the quality, and the polish of the music created there. My level was nothing compared to the average performer. Today, I'm an instrumentalist, and I can put a lot more of my ideas into practice. That's a win. I started to have more contact with other instrumentalists, I'd go to every festival, I'd set up my tent. I moved from the stage to the audience, which, in a way, was fundamental to absorbing all that.*

Another factor that was fundamental for Gil's musical development in London was his ability to form his own band and adopt a different persona on stage [2007]:

I started playing the electric guitar and I contemplated the possibilities of adopting a band leader persona, something that didn't exist during the "bar stool and acoustic guitar" phase that prevailed before Tropicalism. This actually made it possible to utilize certain elements of international pop that were coveted, but out of reach during the Tropicalist phase. Elements of bad technique in singing, composition, instrumentation, accompaniment, the relationship between acoustic and electric guitar. Basically, I electrified the band and became a band leader. [In Brazil] we had worked with Os Mutantes and the Beat Boys. In London, we began to form our own bands, with elements of our own choosing, with a selection of instrumental timbres. Being closer to a world that we had admired from afar also helped.

The first band I formed was a trio with Tutty Moreno on drums and Chris Bonett on bass. That's when I started playing electric guitar – right after recording the album in English. We toured with this band. I bought a van and we went around all the rural areas, doing shows in places like Newcastle. There weren't any Brazilians. In London there actually were a few, but outside London there were only one or two. English audiences usually found us strange, because at that time there was a monolithic interest in rock in England. They came out of curiosity, never out of interest. And, at almost every show, I participated alongside other groups, opening shows for the Moody Blues, for example, and Rod Stewart & The Faces.

London, 1969

In London, we frequented three or four bars, the most important and seminal nightclubs for rock music, which included the Marquee Club, Revolution, Speakeasy, and Ronnie Scott's – which had jazz downstairs and rock and roll upstairs. Those were the clubs, along with many others – like the Roundhouse and the Lyceum, where I saw the 1969 Christmas Eve show with Yoko, John Lennon, and the Plastic Ono Band. I went out a lot. I liked playing bongos in the jam sessions at Revolution and Speakeasy. I played with the guitarist from King Crimson and also Dave Gilmour from Pink Floyd. Not to mention Jim Capaldi from Traffic, and Alan White from the Plastic Ono Band. He worked with Lennon and Yoko before he joined Yes. He was a friend, a regular at my house. Terry Reed, a white R&B musician in the tradition of Alexis Korner, and also John Mayall – that was my circle.

The band and the electric guitar afforded me with another dimension, another persona on stage. You go, you run, you dance, you play around. The composition starts to serve these aspects, it starts to incorporate these aspects. And I discovered that I'm an artist at that, at performance, like those guys in rhythm and blues, who pick up a guitar and go up there.

The album is a must. I do it because there's no other way. It was the only way to keep an audience informed on a large scale, on a massive scale. It's what feeds back into the possibility of coming together with the audience again in live performance.

Among Gil's many new experiences in England, one of the most remarkable was participating in the Isle of Wight Festival with Caetano Veloso, Gal Costa, and Nik Turner, the saxophonist and flautist for the English band Hawkwind. According to Nik, "I was amazed to find out later how important these guys were in Brazil. In the summer of 1970, they were just exotic figures in London's underground scene, jamming with Hawkwind and frequenting art galleries, hippie communities, and music festivals. They seemed so enthusiastic, so generous, so eager to play with anyone."

The Brazilians' participation in the Isle of Wight Festival was spur of the moment, and it happened thanks to Claudio Prado, another Brazilian who was living in London at the time. He would remain Gil's lifelong friend, helping Gil elaborate policies for digital culture when the latter became Brazil's Minister of Culture more than 30 years later. In 2010, Claudio Prado described the festival experience [2010]:

The Isle of Wight Festival was the biggest of them all. The major names of the day performed: Leonard Cohen, Miles Davis, The Doors, The Who. It was Jimi Hendrix's last show. Festivals were liberated territories for three, four days of self-government. A politics of ecstasy. It was a liberated territory, where a person earned the right to be naked, to take acid, to have sex. There was no police or anything. A Liberated Autonomous Zone, before Hakim Bey or anyone else had given it a name.

65 |

All of us were at that festival, all the Brazilians who were part of the artistic community in London: Gilberto Gil, Caetano Veloso, Antônio Bivar, Zé Vicente, Gal Costa, the guys from A Bolha – which was the band that accompanied Gal – Rogério Sganzerla, Julius Bressane. There were about 30 people. Arnaldo Brandão, who was from A Bolha, ended up calling it the experience of his life.

As soon as we arrived, I went to the top of the hill to look at that sea of people. There were hundreds of thousands of people. I took my Orange Sunshine, which was premium California acid. An "ideological" acid, nothing commercial. Halfway through the trip, I felt certain that I had to go down the hill, pick up my group, and take them to the stage at the Isle of Wight Festival, because they had to play there. I went back to the tents where we were camping, and the group was getting together to jam. I grabbed a cassette recorder, state-of-the-art technology at the time, and set it to record. We played for an hour: Gil, Caetano, Gal, everyone. Obviously, I put the recorder there to record the sound I wanted to take on stage, to convince the organizers to let us do a show. When the recording was over, I put the recorder under my arm. I didn't tell anyone else. I went toward the stage with the recorder, wearing nothing but a speedo.

I got to the last gate, where I knew I wasn't going to get past. Jimi Hendrix was there on the other side of the fence. So I just stood there watching people, until a guy appeared, and I said to

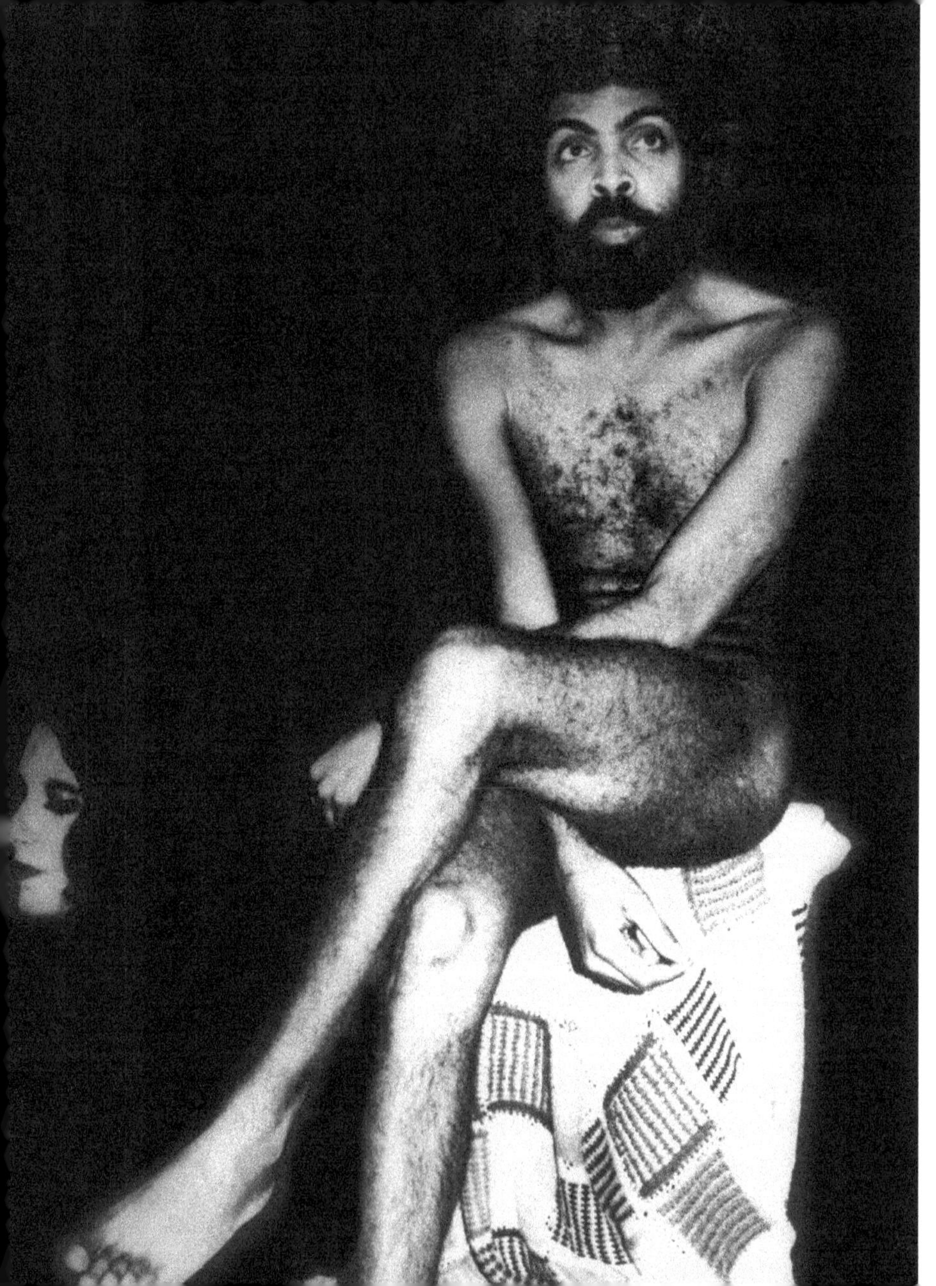

Gil on the set of
the film *Demiurgo*,
by Jorge Mautner,
London, 1971

him: "Look here, look. You're about to go in there, please take this tape recorder and play it for that guy over there." The guy was the presenter.

The guy came back and took me inside. Within seconds I was on stage, talking to the emcee and we were booked to play the next day. I couldn't recreate this conversation; I don't remember it well. But I remember arguing that they were Brazilian musicians, political exiles, and that it would be an important act against the dictatorship for them to perform. He said, "How many of you are there?" I said: "About 30." He said, "You're crazy!" and he gave me a piece of paper authorizing me to enter with 15. I found out the place had two doors, so I got 30 through. I got 15 through at one door, and 15 at the other, with the same piece of paper. A friend of ours, a Belgian sculptor, she'd brought an outfit, a kind of wrinkly red plastic worn by 12 or 13 people with only their faces exposed. It was a walking animal. So I decided to take this on stage. But I arranged for people to be naked underneath, and, at a certain moment, they would get out and dance naked on stage. That all happened, with no planning. It was completely crazy.

The show was Gil on guitar, Caetano, Gal. A friend of ours, Nik Turner – an Englishman who had a totally crazy band, Hawkwind – played the flute and painted himself silver all over. Pericles Cavalcanti was also there: he was part of Caetano's clique. Caetano had that little group of his there, that clique, it was funny. And Gil sang his stuff, Caetano sang his stuff,

*they sang The Beatles. It was acoustic, and it was extremely
pretty, because it was Gil and Caetano in a moment of chaos.
I put the Brazilian flag in front of the stage and I stepped on
it, and I gave a political speech wearing only my red speedo.*

In 1972, Gil returned to Brazil with Sandra Gadelha (to whom
he had been married since 1969) and their son Pedro, who had
been born in exile. In their luggage was the album Gil recorded
in English, as well as the soundtrack to *Copacabana Mon Amour*,
a film by Rogério Sganzerla. Back in Brazil, Gil began working on
Expresso 2222, one of his most important records, which featured
a more refined musical language. In an interview from the time,
he stated [2007]:

*I really think my music is more mature, infused with a
greater number of influences and with a much prettier finish.
Today I have a much greater capacity for polishing work. I
threw a lot in the trash during my experiments in England. I
think 80% of what I did went in the trash. This never happened
before, because the demand exceeded the production capacity.
It was an open-air market atmosphere.*

The new album, produced by Roberto Menescal, benefited
greatly from the musicianship of the backing band, which included excellent performers who had played with Gil previously:
keyboardist Antonio Perna had participated in some shows with

Gil in Bahia in the 1960s; drummer Tutty Moreno and bassist Bruce Henry had played with Gil in London; and guitarist Lanny Gordin, who was part of the Tropicalist group, had worked on the arrangements for Gil's third album alongside Rogério Duprat.

Most of the previously-unreleased songs on the album were written during Gil's time in Europe, including the title track "Expresso 2222," "Oriente," and "O Sonho Acabou". "Back in Bahia" was written after Gil's return to Salvador, as a reflection on the experience of exile: "Today I feel like leaving was necessary / so that I could come back." The album also features two songs originally recorded by Jackson do Pandeiro, "Chiclete com Banana" and "O Canto da Ema."

After recording Expresso 2222, Gil headed out on a national tour with the band. The following years were characterized by constant tours throughout Brazil and by the release of live albums such as *Temporada de Verão* (recorded at the Teatro Vila Velha in 1974 with Caetano and Gal) and *Gil ao Vivo* (from 1975, featuring tracks like "Lugar Comum" and "Abra o Olho"). In 1973, during a performance for the collective show *Phono 73*, censors cut the microphones in the middle of a performance by Gil and Chico Buarque. Their song "Cálice" had been composed specially for the occasion, with a play on words (the song's title, *cálice*, or "chalice," sounds identical to *cale-se*, or "shut up"). The song was subsequently banned, and only released in 1978.

Between 1973 and 1974, Gil began work on a new studio recording, the two-volume album *Cidade de Salvador*. The album was only released in full in 1999, but many of the songs were released in the 1970s as singles, including "Meio de Campo," "Eu Só Quero Um Xodó" (with Dominguinhos), "Eu Preciso Aprender a Só Ser," and "Maracatu Atômico" (by Jorge Mautner and Nelson Jacobina). In 1975, Gil recorded another double album in collaboration with Jorge Ben, *Ogum Xangô*, as well as the first LP of what became known as "The 'Re' Trilogy" – *Refazenda*.[20] The latter LP was released as part of a major tour that passed through more than 100 Brazilian cities. At the time, *Pop* magazine published a beautiful article about the album's creation [1975]:

> *Gilberto Gil was in Bahia after a tour of several capitals and rural cities. One night, he dreamed about the word Refazenda and the somewhat confused image of a farm tucked in a valley with cows, chickens, and trees, but, at the same time, surrounded by a technological apparatus typical of big cities. "It was a place of all people and, at the same time, total solitude. Analyzing it later, I interpreted all that as the synthesis of simplicity, and as a great existential necessity weighing on my mind. I decided to explore the word Refazenda as much as possible, because I think it's very beautiful." Through the*

20. Derived from the Portuguese word for "farm" (fazenda), the neologism Refazenda (re-farm) also suggests action – making or doing over (refazendo), cultivating anew.

formal dissection of the word and from the concept of Refa-zenda, the new LP emerged, along with the direction of Gil's current work: "It's a very simple, quiet, and peaceful LP. The songs are all presented very carefully, without improvisations and without the somewhat absurd vocal experimentation that I now allow myself to do. I never took advantage before. I'm a direct disciple of Luiz Gonzaga and Dorival Caymmi. But, on the other hand, I've made forays into experimentalism, dodeca-phonism, I've used all the oscillators, I've been a troubadour and also Jimi Hendrix."

But as a concept, what does Gil's new work mean? What is Refazenda? "Refazenda is, for me, like a conceptual award for everything I did, was, and will be. My intention is to accentuate this opening, to try to give more color to the green of the jun-gles and make everything be reborn again: so that the flowers return to the fields and the city becomes Refazenda. In short, Refazenda is whatever I want to live, to farm, to go in reverse."

On the other hand, Refazenda is also a timely gesture suggesting a return to simplicity and a return to nature – a new proposal for ecological balance. In explaining the concept in writing, Gil says: "Lace woven with corn tassels, golden corn, corn sun (...) Hope transmuted into veritable verdant green, green magic notes, the charm of the new farm. Re-en-chantment. The tree of the trinity: avocado, tomato, papaya. Miraculous tree: a different fruit every season. (...) Refazenda remains God's will for each season."

Much of this idea was born from Gil's own work – the tireless work of exchanging information – that he intends to continue: "I want to go out there and get to know small towns in the interior, taking shows to people who are in much greater need of a world of dreams and fantasy – whether a show by Gilberto Gil or any other artist. One of these performances is much denser than the Rio-São Paulo circuit. Someone must do this work of taking art to the interior. As a matter of fact, since I came back from England, I've dedicated myself to this."

And Refazenda "must be in the city too." Or in the mind of each and every person, even if it leads to mysticism. "I consider myself a mystic par excellence. I've already gotten familiar with all the religious sects in search of knowledge, in search of a better balance between matter and spirit, heaven and earth: Candomblé, Zen-Buddhism, yoga, etc. Every new phase is a voluntary prison I submitted myself to in search of freedom, you feel me? Refazenda begins in a valley and ends at the limits of the mind…"

In 1976, Gil joined Caetano, Gal, and Maria Bethânia to form Os Doces Bárbaros, an homage to the loosely-knit *grupo baiano* or Bahian group they were part of 10 years prior. In June, the group set out on a tour of several Brazilian cities that eventually became a film by Jom Tob Azulay and a live double album recorded at the Canecão in Rio de Janeiro. But the tour was interrupted by police repression. After a concert in the southern state of Santa

Catarina on July 7th, Gil and drummer Chiquinho Azevedo were arrested for possession of marijuana. In an interview with journalist Nelson Motta at the time, Caetano talked about the tour and the arrests [1980]:

> *While we were on our way to Galeão [Airport in Rio], singer Elizeth Cardoso's car drove up alongside ours. She smiled at us and waved. We set out on our Doces Bárbaros tour blessed. It's not often that we're able to harmonize so many different energies into a clear light. And it's not easy. But that's what Gilberto Gil, Maria Bethânia, Gal Costa, and I are achieving now. We have no intention of creating or solving problems, or of getting into fights. Bob Marley: "Don't deal with dark things." João Donato and Jorge Ben, people who rediscovered faith. With simplicity, we show the music and poetry of life, of everything that is living – the Orixás [divinities of Candomblé]; good, beautiful, and strong people; the fish – and of hope. Within our immediate circumstances, our work is good. It's what we have. And the rest, is the rest.*
>
> *For example, the city of Florianópolis (the name given to the city of Desterro[21]) isn't supposed to be on our tour, because the production team didn't think it would be lucrative (180,000*

21. The colonial settlement located on what is now the island of Florianópolis was known as Our Lady of Exile, or simply, Exile.

inhabitants). At Gil's and my insistence, it got added to the list. Gal didn't want to go, and Bethânia had a sort of premonition that going there wouldn't be good. When the police interrupted our sleep and our joy, I told Gal: "Looks like we were a little too devil-may-care about coming to Florianópolis, and it got to the police chief." Indeed, my acquaintances there told me: "I didn't believe you were coming until I saw you." One even asked me: "Why did you include Florianópolis on the schedule?" – "Out of love," I replied.

The police entered the apartment of Gal Costa, Maria Bethânia, Lea Millon, Eunice Oliveira, Maria Pia de Araújo, Guilherme Araújo, Chiquinho Azevedo, Djalma Correa, Arnaldo Brandão, Perinho Santana, Caetano Veloso, Gilberto Gil, Tuzé de Abreu, Mauro Senise, Tomás Improta, Daniel, as well as the apartment of the sound, light, and stage technicians. They claimed they had received a complaint from [the city of] Curitiba. Against whom? Against all these people? They managed to take Gil and Chiquinho. We didn't set out to debate laws or morals. Nor religion, politics, or aesthetics. We set out to avoid arguing, and we won't argue. We set out filled with the light of life, with love in our hearts. It's not often someone is able to say this, but I'll say that we are a group of people who are out there working for the Good. And anyone in the police, the press, or in hell who wants to attack or hinder us, they will be working for the Bad.

Os Doces Bárbaros:
Caetano, Bethânia,
Gal and Gil, 1976

Gil and Chiquinho were sent to a psychiatric institute near Florianópolis where they remained for two weeks before being released and taken to Rio. They were then forced to undergo outpatient treatment at the Sanatório Botafogo. Despite the fact that the police wanted to make these musicians into examples of how to combat the use of and supposed addiction to drugs, Gil demonstrated courage in maintaining his ideological commitment to the legalization of marijuana. João Santana, a Bahian journalist then known as Patinhas (who would later become famous as a campaign organizer for the Brazilian Workers' Party), wrote a long article following Gil's arrest, in which he stated "Pot is neither God nor the devil." In an interview with Santana, Gil stated [2007]:

After trying marijuana, I really started to use it. I was able to really smooth out certain edges I found in my being, in my personality. I was able to face the fear of the world and the fear of life. In other words, it became an ally of mine, as Carlos Castañeda says. Meaning that it enabled me to see certain things better, to position myself better in the face of the complexity of the world today. So I can't continue lying. It doesn't make sense for me to keep saying that "it's an evil," because of the children or whatever.

I know that drugs have this more cautious, more dangerous character, because they act directly on the creative idea center, on the creative center of humanity's destiny. In other words, the mind is the way humanity guides itself, the mind is the center of everything. So maybe a lot more attention is paid to the effect of drugs on the mind than to the effect of mangoes on the blood.

Now, it's a question of values, too. Me, for example, I followed a macrobiotic diet and I learned that the body is the temple of the spirit. So I attach great importance to my body. For me, during certain periods, it was much more dangerous to eat super-processed things, to eat preserved foods that contain carcinogens, than to smoke marijuana. I knew one thing was going to do me a lot of harm, more harm than the other. It's up to each person.

In contrast to the first time he was arrested in 1968, Gil was now alert and strong, prepared to face the situation with his head held high. Years later, he would declare: "Prison was traumatic, but my insistence on telling the truth became instructive and today it is part of the history of MPB."

Before long, Gil was back on the road. The doctor who examined him at the clinic in Rio had prescribed him "work therapy." It couldn't be better: he resumed the *Refazenda* tour, which crisscrossed nearly the entire nation. In early 1977, he traveled with Caetano Veloso to Lagos, Nigeria, to participate in the Second Festival of Black Art and Culture. For Gil, getting in touch with African culture was a transformative experience, one that would develop into his next album, *Refavela*, the second installation in the "Re" trilogy.

Upon his return from the festival, Gil gave a long interview with the newspaper *Invasão*. He talked about what he witnessed at the festival, which had included performances by artists and groups from several African countries, including Angola, Mozambique, the Congo, and Ivory Coast. He described the conflict between economic poverty and cultural wealth [2007]:

> *The basic substance of the festival in Nigeria, of being there, was seeing all that ethnic stuff, which was really interesting for us. Observing Africa as humanity, right? Observing mankind's way of being there, as a race, as a search-for-being. Observing the fact that, this thing which could be called religiosity in my music and which revolves around Blackness, for them is not seen on that level. Meaning that what we call African religiosity for them is life. Candomblé, the ritualism of the tribes, and the mystical character of tribal life are everyday things for them.*
>
> *For me, the experience was, as Juscelino used to say, 50 years [of progress] in five.[22] This festival in Nigeria was like living 10 years in a month. The emblematic thing about the festival for them, its chosen meaning, was the effort – the effort of organizing to make it work. And that really was commendable. It was beautiful to see. All of it was very important to them too.*

22. Juscelino Kubitschek, 21st president of Brazil, credited with building the federal capital of Brasília from scratch and promising "50 years of progress in five"

It was important to them to document it through every possible means – the press, television – and to find out how Africa is reflected in Brazil, in the United States, in Latin America, to find out how people talk about African culture outside Africa.

And Africa is a huge reservoir. You see, when Modern Art started, it was there. Modern painting and such, you can see, it's all there in Africa. There's nothing new in Picasso, nothing, nothing, nothing. He just copies everything that had already been done there in its entirety. Modern music, it's all there in Africa. Modern theater, modern set design, bodily expression. So that's how it is, it's a huge reservoir.

To clear this up… it will take a lot of time. It's there, brand new. The soul you see is young, innocent, childlike.

Gil's album *Refavela*[23] shows the influence of his experience in Africa, as well as the influence of the Black cultural resurgence in Brazil during the 1970s. One hears not only African instruments, rhythms, and timbres, but also the sounds of afoxé groups like Ilê Aiyê[24] who were consolidating themselves in Salvador; the funk-influenced sounds of the Black Rio movement which was taking over Rio de Janeiro urban culture; and the political and

---

23. From the word for a Brazilian hillside slum or shantytown, whose population is often disproportionately Afro-Brazilian.
24. Afoxé is the name given to certain percussion troupes, typically associated with Candomblé houses, that processed during Carnival.

social consciousness of the MNU, the Movimento Negro Unificado (United Black Movement). Over time, Refavela has come to be seen as a high water mark not only in Gil's work, but in all of MPB.

Gil explained his view of the album in an interview with Ana Maria Bahiana around the time of its release [2007]:

> The album Refavela *ended up being very much about the concept itself, about this thing of art from the Tropics, about the way Black communities contribute to the formation of new ethnicities and new cultures in the New World, in Brazil, the Caribbean, Nigeria, the United States... All these things, these emerging cultures are characterized by the strong presence of Blackness. I'd say 60 to 70% of the album ended up revolving around this, around this vision of this universe.*
>
> *I wanted the album to have a direct, simple ideology, which is my own, expressed in this confessional mode connected to my existential state. It seems like this started with* Expresso 2222, *and it's been noticeable in all my recent albums... The press claim that this is the most ideological of my records, but I wouldn't call it ideological so much as thematic – this Black, Black youth, Black Rio thing...*
>
> *The record has an element of reportage that focuses on Black urban populations. There's also the song "Ilê-Aye," which is the song of a Black [carnival] association in Bahia... "We're crazy criollos / We're really cool / We have kinky hair / We're Black Power"... That's ideological in tone. But what I'd like to*

Although *Refavela* was exquisite in terms of composition and
arrangements, Gil always had mixed feelings about the final result,
especially in relation to the engineering. Technical quality became
an abiding concern in his artistic work. It came to the forefront
even more when he recorded the album *Nightingale* abroad. The
idea for the album was born following Gil's brilliant performance
at the Montreux festival in Switzerland. Gil was accompanied by
the band A Cor do Som, by guitarist Pepeu Gomes, and by percussionist Djalma Corrêa. The performance spurred Gil to pursue
an international career.

Gil moved to Los Angeles with his family for a year. There,
he recorded the album *Nightingale*, produced by Sérgio Mendes,
and released as part of a tour of several cities. Although Gil's
international career did not take off at that time, the album con-

tained two important developments: a more technically-refined studio sound, as well as more of a pop sound influenced by the musicians he met in the United States [2007]:

> *With* Nightingale, *I met Michael Sambello, Stevie Wonder, Nathan East, and Abe Laboriel, all those people who were already around, and who would later come to occupy the noble space of California pop music, characterized by the fusion of pop and rock that was just starting at that time. And so with this record, I was very moved, very stimulated by this kind of thing. It was still very fresh for me when I went on to make the album* Realce, *right after that.*

Realce, the album that closes the "Re" trilogy, became one of Gil's greatest hits. Released in 1979, it features a highly danceable sound, as well as the song "Não Chore Mais," an adaptation of Bob Marley's "No Woman, No Cry." The song became an anthem for the Brazilian political opening that eventually ended with a return to democracy. The song was the best-selling single of Gil's career, with more than 750,000 copies sold. It also represents a consolidation of Gil's affinity with reggae, which he first encountered in London while frequenting the Jamaican cultural scene in Portobello. In 1980, Gil even performed with Jimmy Cliff, another big name in reggae. And in 2001, he would release the album *Kaya N'Gan Daya*, in homage to Bob Marley.

In 1979, Gil separated from Sandra Gadelha, with whom he had had three children (Pedro, Preta, and Maria). He began what would become a long-lasting relationship with his current wife, Flora Giordano, who also became Gil's manager. Gil and Flora had three children together, Bem, Bela, and José.

In 1981, Gil released the album *Luar – A Gente Precisa Ver O Luar* (Moonlight – We Need to See the Moonlight) which features hits such as the title track, as well as "Palco" and "Se Eu Quiser Falar Com Deus." The album kicked off a long partnership with the producer Liminha, who would remain his producer for most of his subsequent albums. The two already knew each other from the days when Liminha was the bassist for Os Mutantes. Liminha became a major Brazilian producer in the 1980s, actively participating in several seminal Brazilian rock albums. In 1984, Gil and Liminha founded the studio Nas Nuvens in Rio's Jardim Botânico neighborhood where Gil recorded his subsequent albums.

The albums Gil released during the 1980s were marked by greater pop influence. These records endeared him to a broader audience, and included *Um Banda Um* (1982), with the hits "Andar Com Fé" and "Esotérico"; *Extra* (1983); *Raça Humana* (1984), with the hits "Tempo Rei" and "Vamos Fugir" (the latter song recorded in Jamaica with the participation of The Wailers); *Dia Dorim Noite Neon* (1985); and *O Eterno Deus Mu Dança* (1989).

But the 1980s were also a time of acute existential crisis for Gil. In a 1982 interview with Regina Echeverria, Gil, always courageous, shared his inner turmoil with the public [2007]:

Dominguinhos, Luiz Gonzaga
and Gilberto Gil, 1980s

Every person has a heightened concern with the appearance of well-being, with that which signifies tranquility, joy, pleasure. In the case of the artist, even more so, I think. There is a certain concern – who knows, maybe a need – for artists to demonstrate that they're doing well, that life is wonderful, that their work is going great, that everything is great. Maintaining the image, not disappointing the public, not hurting the fans… there's that whole thing. After all, it could hurt your career [to have people saying] "What's going on with Gil?" "He's not doing well." This concern isn't just the trivial problem of image; it's that the artist doesn't like to admit to a lot in public. But I think at a certain point you can't get hung up on this. You really aren't superman. The artist has to manage their inner turmoil like anyone else.

When I talked about experiencing a "breakdown of intellectual muscle tone," I received three or four phone calls and even letters from concerned friends. But we're also entitled to use the metaphors we want. I think what's happening to me can actually be seen as a breakdown. If you don't have preferences, if you don't have standards, if you don't have energy, initiative, if you can't get out of a certain limbo, a certain purgatory, you have to admit that there's something like a breakdown happening there.

The question of success was important in this case. Success cannot be a burden. It's the byproduct of a pseudo-commitment that looks like a commitment, but isn't. Each album is

*an experience that is used up in itself. Selling more, becoming
a success – it's a joke. But success or non-success is a part of
every artist's life. So you always have to be right in the middle.
You can't go too far one way or the other: sell records or don't
sell records. This is an absurd formulation for an artist. Hence
Caetano's complaint about Simone and Fagner. It's so silly to
say "It's only worthwhile if you sell a million records." It's the
same thing as saying you don't want to sell records, like many
purist quote-unquote artists out there say. All of this is sectar-
ianism, naivety, ideological disease, ideological hypertrophy.*

Not only did Gil manage to overcome the crisis and continue
composing and recording; the restlessness that provoked the crisis
had another positive outcome. For the first time, Gil decided to
split his time between artistic pursuits and political work. In 1987,
Gil became president of the Gregório de Mattos Foundation, a sort
of municipal Culture Ministry for the city of Salvador, following
an invitation from the then-mayor of the city, Mário Kertész. In
an interview at the time, Gil said [2007]:

*Actually, this had already crossed my mind. Recently I've
felt a desire to participate in political issues and public affairs
creeping in. Mário Kertész and his advisors heard about that.
They're people with whom I have connections (Mário and I
were classmates). He took it into consideration, and I didn't
hesitate. I was already wanting this. I think this impulse has*

to do with the passage of time. This kind of work has been in-sinuating itself into my natural life trajectory. Here and there, you find moments of leadership, of this managerial attitude. There's some of that in my personality.

Gregório de Mattos is a cultural foundation that discusses, plans, and facilitates cultural activities. It's existed for almost a year and it seeks to become a cultural mover. It needs a certain dynamism to be able to operate in the community, to entice companies and distribute funds, to deal with the Federal Government. It will also have to accompany the organic development of Salvador. We want all of this to give Bahia back its important role in Brazilian culture. This was a feature of Bahia that was acknowledged by all of Brazilian society, but it has been emptied out. It's more or less like the Mário Kertész administration says: "Salvador, Heart of Brazil." That heart needs to beat strongly in order to pulse blood across the entire Brazilian periphery.

During his term, Gil created an initiative to bring Bahia closer together with African culture by opening the "Casa de Benin" in Salvador and the "Casa da Bahia" in Benin, West Africa. In addition, Gil invited the Italian-born modernist architect Lina Bo Bardi to lead an important revitalization project in Salvador's city center. Above all else, there was an emphasis on unifying reflection and action, the poetic and the political [2007]:

In 1988, Gil decided to take a bigger leap into politics, leaving the Foundation and announcing his intentions to run for mayor of Salvador. However, Gil was passed over by the political party establishment, so he decided to run for City Council instead. He was elected with the highest number of votes in the city. As a member of City Council, Gil became chair of the Environmental Conservation Committee and began to focus more and more on ecological issues. In 1989, he founded Onda Azul, a non-governmental organization focused on ocean conservation.

The turn of the decade was marked by a traumatic event: Gil's son Pedro died on February 2, 1990, after a car accident. He was 19 years old and he was the drummer in Gil's band. Gil later recalled with great beauty how he had dealt with the death of his son [2007]:

It was a brutal shock, a fright that took a toll on my physical and mental well-being. In recent years, I've experienced a great deal of memory loss, and my friends attribute the acceleration of this process to Pedro's death. But I think about him with stillness. I've dreamed about him a few times. It gave me tremendous pleasure to see him, without the joy of knowing he was alive. I had the pain of knowing he was dead, but without suffering, since he was alive in my memory.

During the early 1990s, Gil continued to compose. In 1992, he recorded *Parabolicamará*. The title track is an impressive reflection on the possibilities and challenges of globalization: "The world used to be small / Because the Earth was big / Today the world is very big / Because the Earth is small / The size of the parabolicamará antenna / Around the world, camará / The world goes round, camará" [2007]:

I called the album Parabolicamará, naming some of the aspects of a possible globalization that I envisioned and even desired, in a way that was both joyful and tragic, like someone who deeply desires everything that happens to him. Parabolicamará unites the words "parabolic" – from the antenna that today is ubiquitous throughout the poorest corners of Brazil – with "camará" – from the way practitioners of capoeira, the Afro-Brazilian fight game, call their partners "comrades" while dancing and singing.

In the years that followed, Gil focused on two special projects. In 1993, in partnership with Caetano Veloso, he released the album *Tropicália 2* in celebration of the movement's 25th anniversary. The album includes some formal experimentation, as well as several songs that would become part of the artists' regular repertoire, such as the overtly political song "Haiti" and the beautiful "Desde Que O Samba É Samba."

The album generated some controversy for having omitted the other musicians and artists who were part of the original Tropicália moment. But according to Gil [2007],

Caetano was saying clearly: "Look, there are many requests to commemorate Tropicália, in different ways and in different contexts. Let's make a record, so we can be free of everything else!" And so it was decided that we would make the record together. Caetano said: "Tropicalia 2, let's focus on the two of us!" That was his choice too. It was a radicalization, since the celebrations could have turned into various events and subgroups.

Tropicália 2, as a broad manifesto, is a reaffirmation of the belief in freedom and plurality. It's a democratic record. The album joins forces with those who are building the future. Anything less is not enough. On the individual level, it's a reaffirmation of origins – the sertão, the baião, the samba de roda from Bahia, my Afro-Bahian expressiveness, the American songs I used to listen to as a child, 1960s pop – as with the re-recording of Jimi Hendrix's "Wait Until Tomorrow." In an intimate sense, it's a nostalgic record of reminiscences.

In 1994, Gil recorded a live acoustic album, *Unplugged*, in a special event for MTV Brasil. The performance was similar to the one the network had previously done with Eric Clapton in the United States. With a backing band comprised of musicians such as Celso Fonseca (guitar), Arthur Maia (bass), Jorginho Gomes (drums), Lucas Santtana (flute), and Marcos Suzano (percussion), the album features impeccable execution. The repertory not only included some of Gil's greatest hits, it also revived songs that had been hidden on their original records, such as "Drão" and "Esotérico," and included the theme music Gil composed for the educational children's TV show "Sítio do Pica-Pau Amarelo." The album was one of the biggest commercial successes of Gil's career and introduced his work to a new generation of listeners.

In the second half of the 1990s, Gil began to experience some vocal difficulties that required him to change the keys of some songs on later albums and shows [2007]:

The main cause is that 15, 20 years ago, I abused my voice. I screamed a lot. I used my voice as an instrument of improvisation and dedicated myself to bold experimentation, without technical guidance and assistance. I ended up forming two small nodules, one on the right-hand vocal cord, the other on the left, which caused me to become hoarse easily, and to lose some vocal quality. It's a simple and benign thing. There's no medical recommendation for surgical intervention. For a year I've been treating it with homeopathy and speech therapy exercises with great results. I still have a kind of velvety layer around my voice, but it's not quite hoarse, nor does it stop me from singing and hitting the notes demanded by the songs. I'm starting to "contralto" my voice a little more, trading the higher soprano regions for a more contralto voice. This tendency toward lower notes is related to age. It happens to all singers who get older. The vocal cords no longer have the same elasticity. So, one of the easy fixes is to lower the keys.

Health challenges did not keep Gil from one of his best creative phases, however. He intensified his focus on new technologies and on the relationship between science and art in his next album, *Quanta*, from 1997. According to Gil, *Quanta* is his most conceptual album, and this presented some challenges for him during production [2007]:

> Quanta *is a poetic reading of science and its interfaces with philosophy, religion, and art. My goal on the record is to create bridges between the magical field and the field of physics, to depict a certain proximity between science and mysticism. Ever since Tropicalism, this was the idea – to create bridges between universes. I made this a habit. That's why I say I'm a Tropicalist to this day.*

The second track on the album, "Ciência e Arte" (Science and Art), was written by the "old guard" samba artists Cartola and Carlos Cachaça. It was the lyricist Carlos Rennó who introduced the song to Gil. According to Gil, "it is an intricate, poetic samba story dedicated to praising the sciences and other fields of knowledge in Brazil. It's the album's flagship song."

After the album was already finished, Gil decided to update later editions with one final track, created in collaboration with Caetano's son Moreno Veloso, as well as Lucas Santtana. The track is a collage of music and text, from indigenous songs to punk rock. The piece dialogues directly with the Tropicalist song "Objeto Semi-Identificado" ("Semi-Identified Object") and is titled "Objeto Ainda Menos Identificado" ("Even-Less-Identified Object").

Quanta was very well received. The album was considered a return to Gil's most experimental period of the 1960s, and it yielded a successful tour and a live album, *Quanta Gente Veio Ver*, released the following year. In this way, Gil ended the 1990s with a bang. The next decade would bring new challenges: Gil resumed his political activity and in 2003 he became the Minister of Culture under President Luiz Inácio Lula da Silva. His term as minister from 2003 to 2008 was characterized by the strengthening of the Ministry of Culture, and by a series of innovative policies that revolved around digital culture and the creation of what were known as Culture Points (Pontos de Cultura). In his inaugural speech, Gil proposed the concept of an "anthropological do-in"[24] that would guide his efforts at invigorating the existing cultural spaces across the country [2013]:

95 |

> *What I mean by "culture" extends far beyond the limited and limiting scope of academic concepts and the liturgical rites of a so-called "artistic and intellectual class." Culture, as someone once said, is not just "a kind of ignorance that distinguishes scholars." Nor is it simply that which is produced within the scope of those forms that are already canonized by Western codes, with their suspect hierarchies.*
>
> *Furthermore, no one will hear me say the word "folklore." The links between the scholarly concept of "folklore" and cultural discrimination are more than close. They are intimate.*

24. From the Eastern acupressure or self-massage technique do-in.

"Folklore" is everything that – having failed to fit within the panorama of mass culture due to its antiquity – is produced by unrefined people, by "contemporary primitives." Like some kind of archaic symbolic reservoir in the contemporary world. Lina Bo Bardi's teachings definitively warned me about this trap. There's no such thing as "folklore" – what exists is culture.

Culture is everything that manifests beyond mere use-value whenever we use something. Culture as that which transcends the merely technical, in each object we produce; culture as a symbol generator of a people; culture as the set of signs belonging to each community and nation; culture as the meaning of our actions, the sum of our gestures, the sense of our behavior. From this perspective, the actions of the Ministry of Culture should be understood as exercises in applied anthropology. The Ministry must be like a light that reveals the things and signs that made and make Brazil, Brazil, both in the past and in the present. Thus, the stamp of culture, the lens of culture, will be applied to everything that reveals and expresses, so that we can weave the thread to hold them together. It is not the State's place to create culture, but rather to create the conditions for universal access to symbolic goods. It is not the State's place to create culture, but rather to provide the necessary conditions for the creation and production of cultural goods, whether artifacts or mind-facts [mentefatos]. *It is not the State's place to create culture, but rather to promote the general cultural development of society.*

Access to culture is a basic right of citizenship, along with the right to education, healthcare, and a healthy environment. By investing in the conditions for creation and production, we will be taking up an initiative with unpredictable but certainly brilliant and profound consequences. From early colonial times to now, Brazilian popular creativity has always far exceeded what the educational, social, and economic conditions of our existence allowed. In fact, the State has never been at the same level as our people in any of the diverse branches of the great tree of Brazilian symbolic creation.

But at the same time, the Ministry cannot be just a fund transfer system for a preferred clientele. So I have to offer the caveat: it is not the State's place to create culture, except in one very specific and inevitable sense – in the sense that formulating public policies for culture is also producing culture; in the sense that every cultural policy is part of the political culture of a society and of the people, at a given moment of existence; in the sense that any cultural policy cannot help but express essential aspects of the culture of these people.

But also in the sense that it is necessary to intervene. Not according to the old statist model, but in order to clear paths, open clearings, stimulate, and shelter. To enact a kind of anthropological "do-in" by massaging vital points that might be momentarily neglected or dormant within the cultural body of the country. In short, to enliven the old and stir up the new. Brazilian culture cannot be thought of outside this

For any attentive listener, the intimate coherence between Gil's cultural policy proposal and his own musical work is undeniable. Both revolve around openness, plurality, and the complex ability to deal with different fields of expression. As Culture Minister, Gil also brought the debate around digital culture to the world in an innovative way, namely, through the debate around authorship and copyright. This concern brought him into alignment with initiatives such as Creative Commons. In an interview conducted by Rodrigo Savazoni and myself for the book *Cultura Digital. br*, in partnership with the Ministry of Culture, Gil analyzed the impact and challenge of the digital within the cultural sphere. He remained hopeful about the possibilities for the democratization of culture [2009]:

sion – all these things are affected by digital life, because of the considerable increase in accessibility and in symbolic exchanges that the digital world offers. It's a new world, particularly because of accessibility, speed, widespread use, and the penetration of use into spheres previously controlled by few groups. Specialists who dominated a particular field cease to monopolize that domain. Now there's cross-training, multi-use, all the things the digital world provides. It's a world that also socialized all the tools and that streamlined functional intelligence, which is how intelligences come into play in dialogue with instrumentality. All of this is affected by digitality. It's like we've moved into a new culture. Everything got very fast and very broad.

The thing that still prevents music, culture, and cultural activities from flooding the world thanks to this lack of differentiation between those who consume-produce and those who produce-consume, is the issue of remuneration for the product, and the continued necessity of framing the cultural good, the cultural service, in terms of goods and services. It's been that way for the entire life of capitalism and for the entire productive life of our society, and it may now change from the standpoint of authorship. This technological flood is inevitable, and what happens to it will depend on how the system reacts. The system still lives from the possibility of paying and getting paid. Enterprises are all based on this double function, and the system will fight really hard to maintain the possibility of a business dimension of life. As long as this exists, there will always be an attempt to contain this flood. But the digital world brings virtuality and reality together. Everything gets very confused, and it is difficult to contain this flood.

The presence of an artist like Gil at the head of the Ministry of Culture was not only important domestically, but also internationally. Gil's performance at a 2003 meeting of the United Nations is proof of this. The event was a celebration of International Peace Day, as well as a tribute to those killed in an attack on a UN building in Baghdad a short time before. That attack left 24 dead, including Brazilian ambassador Sérgio Vieira de Mello. During his presentation, Gil invited then-UN General Secretary and Nobel Peace Prize Laureate Kofi Annan on stage to play drums in the song "Toda Menina Baiana." The encounter was heavily symbolic, as Gil reminded us [2017]:

That was an example of trans-institutional diplomacy, at the Plenary of the United Nations in New York, in front of hundreds of diplomats representing the various nations of the world. We had an artist from one nation with a very strong reputation for cultural activity, which is Brazil. An artist like this encounters this international diplomatic world and shares the stage with the United Nations' General Secretary, who is an African, and therefore has many features that are naturally associated with Brazilians, Bahians, that artist – in this case,

**Gil performing at the UN
with Kofi Annan, 2003**

There, on the main stage of world politics, was the promise of a Brazil with the potential to become an international presence through culture. In that plenary, we saw a proposal for political action based on joy, art, and the sharing of experiences. The Ministry of Culture under Gil was distinguished by the fact that it elaborated the most radical vision for society within a government that itself proposed "a Brazil for everyone." Gil was, as Caetano put it, "Lula's Lula".

Gilberto Gil remained in the Ministry until 2008, when he was replaced by Juca Ferreira, who had served as his Executive Secretary. Gil left behind the most thorough and well-designed proposal for cultural policy that Brazil has ever had, one that placed the country on the international cutting edge. But, in 2011, with the transition to a new presidential administration, the project was shelved. The proposals remain as a beacon to guide future initiatives.

Following his departure from the Culture Ministry, Gil remained active in the sphere of musical production. He released several albums, including *Banda Larga Cordel* (2008), *Fé na Festa* (2010), *Gilbertos Samba* (2014), and *Ok Ok Ok* (2019). These projects were characterized by reflections on the theme of time and by the pleasure of playing music while surrounded by family. Gil also remained active in public debates, discussing poignant issues of the time. But as he explained in the title track of his 2019 album, Gil also knows when to be silent. The lyrics provide a portrait of wisdom in the face of the hollow and polarized political debate at the time:

> *Ok Ok Ok / I already know you want my opinion / Straight talk about what I thought / How I interpret such a vile situation // Deprivation, fury, clamor, disenchantment / Hard-to-chew nouns / While the rats gnaw on power / The hearts of the weeping crowd / Some suggest I go out screaming / Others, that I keep quiet and mute / And that's when someone asks me to "embody the myth" / "Be our hero, solve everything" // Ok Ok Ok / I already know you want my opinion / Straight talk about what I thought / How I interpret such a vile situation // Of the many who prefer me to be silent / Few speak in my favor / Most of them join the angry chorus / Of those who wound me with their hate and terror / As for those who want me to be more active / More sympathetic to the suffering of the poor / I hope my soul is noble enough / As long as I'm alive // Ok Ok Ok / You still want my opinion / Straight talk about what I thought / How I interpret such a vile situation // The truly-noble noble loved his people / Valued care and compassion more / Treated his vassal with affection / The same as the dog and the horse / So me, a musician and poet, I don't speak / I keep silent about certainties and finalities / My straight talk puts on skates / Sliding across targets and goals // Ok Ok Ok / I know I didn't*

give an opinion / It's that I thought, thought, thought, thought
/ Words say yes, the facts say no.

The song is a portrait of two Gil's who coexist. On the one hand is Gil's public persona, the man who never shied away from debate, who always knew what time it was and when to speak out, the icon of a generation of artists who publicly positioned themselves on the political issues of their time, as he himself points out [2018]:

> *We come from a generation of artists and popular musicians who, in a way, inaugurated this thing of being militant in our public opinions, of taking positions on customs, on the existential dimensions of each person, on politics, on the various issues related to social life – myself, Caetano, Chico Buarque, Geraldo Vandré, Milton Nascimento, this group of people from that generation, plus those who came later and strengthened this process of militancy in public opinion. For that very reason, people demand that of us. The expectation is already there, due to the very fact that we're willing to work in this field of public opinion, with derivatives of this classification, as opinion makers. Therefore, the very idea of being an artist demands this of us.*

With the advent of social media which encourages confrontation and polarization, this demand is further amplified. This aspect of the internet is a far cry from the digital utopia that excited Gil in the early days of the digital network [2018]:

> *Society is less and less patient. With the advent of the internet, with these tools for consolidating audiences, collectives, and also individuals within their territories and within their corners, this demand for public posturing and opinion has become even greater. It has intensified a lot in recent years. That's where the great polarizations of today are born, in the radicalization of conflicts between opposites in the field of ideology. Our generation inaugurated this media thing where public opinion circulates through many of our heads. The internet has intensified this, leading to this consolidation.*

Faced with this reality, there is a second Gil who appears in the song "Ok Ok Ok" – the serene Gil who knows when to be silent. This serenity has accompanied him during recent years, as for example when he cast his attentive and expansive gaze on the topic of time [2018]:

> *In the song "A Paz", which I wrote with João Donato, the lyrics say "Only war makes our love in peace." Peace is a choice in the middle of everything, a choice that is made possible first by this desire, this impulse, this work of wanting to finally be at peace, and then, by the fact that it is only possible in the*

midst of so much difficulty, so much failure, so much quarrel, so much difficulty... Only the search for peace can provide balance and pull you out of that pit of despair, out of hopelessness. It's a permanent search and, in many cases, for many people, it's a process of production. You must produce peace. In my case, for example, why did I go to yoga? Why did I seek out spiritual disciplines? Why did I look at various philosophies, those of the East, etc.? It was because I was looking for some clarity about what we are, where we came from, where we're going, and about the meaning of all this. Meaning that this search – this production of peace like I said – is what makes it more concrete and solid as a rock.

The future has become urgent. At 77 years old, the future has become very near, because a lot of things have already become the past in my life. So, the present is the indefinable, the present is here and now, it is immediate and there's nothing to say. It is us, it is this vital fact. Deep vitalism. The future, on the other hand, is the projection and the unfolding. So at the age of 77, the future is right there, in just a little while [laughs]. Beyond that, it remains open. It is no longer what you desire, what you want and build. For me it's no longer about building the future. The only thing now is moving myself in the present toward the permanent meeting with the future. For me now, the future is permanence.

In his 2003 inaugural speech as Minister of Culture, Gil reflected on the history of the nation, and on the the possibility of building the future [2013]:

> *Either Brazil ends violence, or violence ends Brazil. Brazil cannot continue to be synonymous with a great undertaking, but one that is always interrupted, or with an undertaking that is collective in name only. It cannot continue being, as Oswald de Andrade said, a country of slaves who insist on being free men. We must finish building the nation.*

We still don't know what future proposals for resuming the invention of Brazil may look like. In the face of today's violence, we're just starting to incubate the dream of tomorrow. But one thing we can be sure of is that any vision for a generous, collective, comprehensive, and free Brazil will pass, inexorably, through the luminous figure and body of thought of Gilberto Gil.

WORKS CITED

1975. Campos, Augusto de. *Balanço da Bossa*. Perspectiva, São Paulo, 1975.

1975. *Revista Pop*. August 1975.

1980. Motta, Nelson. *Música Humana Música*. Salamandra, Rio de Janeiro, 1980.

1992. Chediak, Almir. *Songbook Gilberto Gil Vol. 2*. Lumiar, Rio de Janeiro, 1992.

2007. Cohn, Sergio. *Gilberto Gil - Encontros*. Azougue, Rio de Janeiro, 2007.

2009. Cohn, Sergio, and Rodrigo Savazoni. *Cultura Digital.br*. Azougue, Rio de Janeiro, 2009.

2010. Cohn, Sergio, Fabio Maleronka and Rodrigo Savazoni. *Produção Cultural no Brasil*. Azougue, Rio de Janeiro, 2010.

2011. Mac Cord, Getúlio. *Tropicália: Um Caldeirão Cultural*. Ferreira Editoria, Rio de Janeiro, 2011.

2012. Terra, Renato. *Uma Noite em 67*. Civilização Brasileira, Rio de Janeiro, 2012.

2013. Gil, Gilberto, and Juca Ferreira. *Cultura Pela Palavra*. Versal, Salvador, 2013.

2017. Leal, Claudio. "Conceituação foi do Caetano, eu tive papel político." *Folha de São Paulo*. April 9, 2017.

2018. Menezes, Thales de. "Gil dá atestado de vida em OK OK OK." *Folha de São Paulo*. August 21, 2018.

"I WANT HUMANITY TO FULFILL ITS PURPOSE"

*Interviews with Leonardo Lichote, 2019 (Projeto Cria)
and Ana Paula Simonaci, Leonardo Lichote,
Paulo Almeida and Sergio Cohn, November 2020*

*Gil, the conversation here at Cria is about the
composition process. So, I always like to start
by asking about the first song you wrote.*

I'd jotted down a lot of things when I played the accordion. I started studying accordion when I was 10 years old. Around my teenage years, I was playing with a group. It was called Os Desafinados ("The Out-of-Tune Ones").

Because of João Gilberto,[1] right?

Right, and so there weren't any compositions yet with parts, art, arrangements, and so forth, but I improvised a lot on the accordion. There's nothing left from that phase. Nothing really transformed or condensed into a song. The first song I ended up writing was after [I learned] the guitar, which I started playing because of João Gilberto. Seduced by João. Before that I couldn't do it. I played accordion, which is all about the scale, with harmonic sequences orga-

1. Bossa nova artist who played the first recorded version of the song "Desafinado."

nized in a Pythagorean way. Everything was very clear. And when I picked up the guitar, I said, "This is really weird." I couldn't understand why one string was like that, and the other... and the other... they formed a chord. Everything was hazy. But eventually I learned to play. I ended up learning because of João.

My first song I remember writing was like this: "If you say / You still want me, love / I'll come running to embrace you / Your kisses, your caresses / I'm always seeking them / The way the poet seeks inspiration / In the moonlit nights // If you say / That you still want me, love / I'll come running to be with you / And united, close together / We'll depart, just the two of us / And the good stuff – happiness – will come next."

Pure bossa nova. Pure João Gilberto. And even the first line is "if you say" (se você disser) like in "Desafinado." But what was it like in Ituaçu before bossa nova?

Well, in Ituaçu, there was the local music, the natural music, the music that happened there because of the pilgrims and the vendors especially. The pilgrims at the market fair. Ituaçu had 800 inhabitants in 1950. In the 1950 census, I was going to be eight years old, and Ituaçu had 800 inhabitants. Therefore, it was [the equivalent of] a block or a small neighborhood in an average city. And that was the local music. At market fairs on Saturdays, the vendors always arrived with loads of brown sugar, flour, beans, rice, fruit, Brazil plum... all those things. And the fair was located there, and they would come. The fair was on Saturday. Some started arriving on Thursday to set up a tent and do all the things.

The fair was... There was a kind of market that was built later when I was born. In 1943, 1944 they built the market, but the habit from before remained, where people would stay around the perimeter of the market. In part because the market couldn't fit everyone in it, with all the vendors and whatnot. They stayed outside the market, they pitched their tents around the perimeter. So some arrived on Thursday night, or on Friday morning, in the afternoon and such, to secure their spot, to pitch their tent. And there was always a guitar player [*violeiro*], right? There was always a guitar player, a singer.

Many of them came too, many singers, many guitar players. Some blind people also came and passed the hat for some change because of the number of people there Saturdays. So that was the first live music I saw, when I was two, three, four years old at the most. I would go to the fair and see a lot of these people playing and singing. Therefore, the songs were related to the region, to all the northeastern Brazilian themes, all that. Ituaçu is part of the arid *caatinga* scrubland. It could be considered part of the Drought Corridor in the Northeast.

And at home I listened to the radio. Rádio Nacional, with several programs that aired all week. Every day there was at least one music program. There was Dalva de Oliveira, the Batista sisters, Jorge Goulart, Nora Ney, and then Angela Maria. Anyway, a long line of important singers. Everything was broadcast from Praça Mauá here [in Rio de Janeiro], you know? In the building A Noite. Rádio Nacional was located there, on the top floor of the building A Noite, and it broadcast from there throughout Brazil. It was one of the most powerful radios at that time, and it reached all of Brazil.

Another radio that also reached [Ituaçu] was Rádio Tupi. And on Rádio Tupi I always listened to *Calouros em Desfile* with Ary Barroso. Ary Barroso presenting the newbies and such. Another radio station that also had quite a lot of power was Mayrink Veiga, but this one didn't have so many musical performances.

And what fascinated you about this?

Ah, everything. I liked everything. All these names I mentioned here, I loved them. And I was already paying special attention to Luiz Gonzaga, because he started on one of Ary Barroso's shows. He went to play for one of the *Calouros em Desfile* programs. They say Gonzaga played a polka, or something like that. And [Ary] said, "What's that?" in that snobbish way of his. It seems he was the one who advised Gonzaga to start using the local repertoire, the northeastern repertoire. Ary Barroso influenced Gonzaga's decision to embrace *baião*, *xaxado*, and *xote*.[2]

Luiz Gonzaga stayed with you your entire life.

Yes, listening to the radio and such. But then the real, definitive fascination with Gonzaga was when I saw him singing in the Praça da Sé in Salvador, with his little trio. Him, Catamilho, and the zabumba player on a stage they set up in the Castro Alves Square. Even in those days, he was already drawing a big crowd. He was the great idol, the great pop artist of the time. He could show up anywhere and fill public squares throughout Brazil. And when I was little, perhaps eight years old, I went to see Gonzaga and I became fascinated. That stuck in my head.

Two years later, a year or so later, there was an accordion school in Salvador founded by a doctor, Dr. José Benito Colmenero, a Spaniard who played bandoneon and accordion. He started this school. It was called Escola de

2. Dance genres associated with rural backlands and forró repertory.

Acordeon Regina, because he was dating Regina, one of the girls who helped teach classes there. And it was because of Gonzaga that I asked my mom to give me an accordion and send me to that school. I went to Colmenero's Accordion Academy.

Gonzaga was so important to me that my nickname at home, among my circle of friends, was "Jiló", because of his song "Qui Nem Jiló."

There's a core element of your guitar-playing that comes from Gonzaga's accordion, isn't there?

There's no doubt about it, no doubt. You listen to "Expresso 2222" and you see the accordion in it, right? And that's a funny thing. The little riff I invented on the guitar for that song intrigued a lot of people – many musicians, colleagues, and so on. I remember John McLaughlin – a very famous guitarist, a great musician – he invited me to do a show with him in Paris, where he had a show with his wife who was also a musician. He heard this introduction to "Expresso 2222" and was intrigued, he wanted to know exactly how it went. And we had fun, I did the show with him, I showed him how it went, and much more. And that impression remains–it's very Gonzaga like. It's an imitation of what was called bellows-play [*jogo de fole*]. The "accordion pant," as he called it in a song.[3]

And João Gilberto would come a little later. He was another fundamental source.

Yes, as was evident in the first song I did. Let's not forget that one of the few songs composed and performed by João is called "Bim Bom", right? "My baião is just that / And there's nothing else, no / My heart just asked like this / Bim bom bim bim bom bom / Bim bom bim bim bom bom." Which is a little like the *zabumba*,[4] right? That's so him, being from Juazeiro, from the backlands of Bahia. It carried the influence of all that music. And he brought that together. So much so that when I went to learn... I bought my guitar... my mother gave me the money to buy it. I went to [the department store] Mesbla and bought a DiGiorgio, a guitar that was quite respectable. I bought the Bandeirante method, the Canhoto method, and I went home to learn.

3. The lyrics of "Vem morena" state "I want to see you swing to the accordion pant until the sun comes up."
4. The bass drum characteristic of northeastern forró music.

So I wanted to do the bossa nova rhythmic pattern, but I couldn't do it, I didn't understand how it worked until I referred back to the *baião*. And when I thought about the *baião*, I could do it. I'm certain that João's rhythmic pattern – maybe even a little unconsciously, but I don't think so, I think he was aware of it – it was something that combined the *baião* and the samba.

And then, decades later, with the reggae thing, there's that funny story with Dominguinhos, who also "referred back" to the baião.

Domiguinhos. We were traveling through the Northeast during the *Refazenda* tour in one of those Chevrolets, I forget the model. I think we were somewhere between Campina Grande and João Pessoa. It was me, Dominguinhos, Chiquinho Azevedo, and whatnot. And I put on a Bob Marley tape, for us to play on the road, like, heading down the road. He listened, listened, listened. When it was over, he said: "Well then, Gil my friend, this is a shameless little *xote*,[5] right?" I said, "Yeah, it is."

5. Slower northeastern dance rhythm characterized by strong backbeat similar to reggae.

He was. But then I was already in love with bossa nova and had already written some songs. I had already done "Felicidade Vem Depois," among others. I was already composing. Belina, my first wife, mother of Nara and Marília, keeps some notebooks of mine where I jotted down songs. The first songs. I was already involved in the music business, when Jorge Ben's *Samba Esquema Novo* (1963) album appeared.

I bought that record at a record store near the Praça da Sé and went home to listen to it. I listened to it one day, two, another entire day, I kept listening, I never stopped listening to that record. I remember meeting up with Caetano a few days later. We were already very close, we were already doing things together. And I said to him: "Look, I'm going to give up. I'm not going to do any more songs or anything like that. I'm going to sing Jorge Ben."

Everything. "Sacundin, sacunden, sacundin, sacunden, sacundaia." The vocal riff thing I absorbed later. All that is Jorge Ben. That's where it comes from, from that thing he does, from that album release. That organic, natural, earthy commitment to Black music. That "Blackish" thing his music has. And for a while I kept... I remember there was a nightclub in Salvador called Boate Clock. They called me one day to do a show and it was during precisely that period. I told them: "I'll do it, but only if I can sing *Samba Esquema Novo* and nothing else." And that was it. I sang all those Jorge Ben songs.

The problem is I don't really know how to imitate his guitar. I managed João Gilberto's, but Jorge Ben's, I can't do it right. Because his is unique, it's personal. It's different, it's a drummed, percussive guitar. Unlike João's, which is a guitar played with the fingers. There's a term for it in Portuguese I don't remember... plangent! A plangent guitar! And Ben's is percussive, there's a pandeiro there.

Well... that's because his origin is also bossa nova. Except that he put in the individualities, the characteristics, the mysteries of each one. He really wanted to create a percussive guitar sound and I had a lot of difficulty doing that, so I didn't incorporate much from it. I went back, I put a stop to that craziness where I wasn't doing my music anymore and was only doing his. I realized that I couldn't compete with Jorge Ben. So, I decided to go back to making my songs my way and then I started to absorb other ways of playing, other ways of strumming the guitar. My guitar-playing is all plucked. It's different.

You worked with jingles early in your career, didn't you?

Yes. I made some jingles, like for a store called Milisam, which was one of the first designer clothes brands in Brazil. And then it became successful. The advertisement played on the radio, people commented. It's funny because that was one of the other things from the non-musical field that had a strong influence on me. The jingle. It left its mark. Many of my songs, even romantic ones, have a jingle feel, from advertising.

*The jingle is the most extreme example of the
issues Tropicália explored conceptually in
relation to commercial or pop music, isn't it?*

Exactly. I remember, Miles Davis – with that voice of his – once I was traveling with him on a plane from Montreux to Nice. He went to Montreux a lot for all those festivals. By chance, I was seated next to him. I had the satisfaction of making that short trip between Switzerland and the south of France on the plane with him. And he chatted with me, one of the things he asked me was: "How's that albino doing?" I said, "Who?" "That albino one." It was about a minute of this, then he said: "Ah, Hermeto Pascoal, of course." I said, "He's doing well, very good." "That albino is formidable." I said, "He is, he's spectacular." And, in the middle of a conversation about music in the United States, at one point he said: "Look, the best thing in music today in the United States is the jingle." Miles Davis, can you imagine?

*What was the emergence of Tropicália like
for you?*

We were already together in Rio, in São Paulo, thinking about Brazilian music. I had lived through bossa nova and the movement to salvage traditional samba. I had performed those memorable shows in Bahia. And then, I took a trip to Recife, to go sing at the Teatro Popular do Nordeste. I received two important invitations. One was to go to Ilha de Itamaraca, where I met Lia de Itamaracá,[7] still a girl, very young, singing the cirandas. One of them is famous and talks about her. "This ciranda was given to me by Lia / Who lives on the island of Itamaracá / I was on the beach / Listening to the crashing waves of the sea." And another invitation was to go to Caruaru, where I met the Banda de Pífanos. Mr. Sebastião Biano is turning 100 years old now. He lives in São Paulo; he's turning 100 years old. Those two visits, those two experiences sent me back to São Paulo with the feeling that we needed to do something. See, it was precisely at that time... I can't remember if I had already listened to *Sgt. Pepper's* before I went to Recife or if I heard it afterwards. But these two things came together, and I said to Caetano: "Caetano, we have to delve into this history of Brazilian music. There are so many elements, so many sources of inspiration, so many sources to draw from, so many motifs and themes and everything else. We need to incorporate it. Bossa nova, okay, it did an extraordinary job, it was a major innovation in Brazilian music, something extraordinary. But we need

7. Famous performer of the folk tradition of ciranda, which involves call-and-response singing in a ring.

to stir something up." That's when we decided to make a move. And you know the story, we invited our friends, all the artists...

Some accepted, others didn't.

Chico [Buarque] says that when we asked him: "Chico, why didn't you want to? You teamed up with everyone else who refused to work with us." He said: "I don't know if I refused anything, Gil. I was completely drunk. I didn't have the ability to accept or refuse. I was completely drunk." But the fact is that our colleagues didn't want to do it because they didn't want to mix English pop music or electric guitar with our stuff. The electric guitar problem was already there.

Yes, and even you went there.

In the march with Elis [Regina], right? The march against the electric guitar. I was completely crazy in love. I went because of her. She organized it; she created the march. And she said to me, in that vehement way, in one of those corridors at TV Record: "Gil, you have to do the march with me." I didn't even... that's it, I went. Except that one month later I had my electric guitar and was playing "Domingo no Parque" with Os Mutantes.

What is your greatest Tropicalist song?

There are several, but let me remember one here, "Marginália II", which I composed with Torquato Neto: "I, Brazilian, confess / My guilt, my sin / My desperate dream / My well-kept secret / My affliction / I, Brazilian, confess / My guilt, my exile / Daily dry bread / Tropical melancholy / Black solitude // Here is the end of the world / Here is the end of the world / Here is the end of the world." And so on. It ends on "here is the end of the world." It was Caetano who asked me to start singing this song again…

The Tropicalist adventure was abruptly interrupted by your arrest and subsequent exile. Caetano says that prison hit him differently than it did you. Prison was a defining moment for you, wasn't it?

Something unusual happened that kind of changed my feelings about it after the fact. Because in prison, it was tough. For him, for me, for Ferreira Gullar, for Paulo Francis, for everyone who was there with us. The group was being held in the barracks. And they brought us in front of the troops to do a ritual shaving of our heads, with our big hair and whatnot. Anyway, it was heavy, being there, the interrogations, that whole thing. "He's a communist, he's not a communist."

But one day Sergeant Juarez came into the cell when I was alone. He says to me: "Do you want a guitar?" I said, "Do you think it's possible?" He said, "I'm going to talk to the commander of the guard," who was a captain whose name I don't remember now. He went and talked to the captain. He came back and said: "Look, I talked to the captain, I'll bring it tomorrow, he let me bring a guitar for you." And he brought a guitar.

So I was able to play guitar and I ended up composing three songs. Actually, four. One of them I completely forgot. Another is "Cérebro Eletrônico," the other is "Futurível," and one is called "Vitrines." They are seminal songs in my repertory. They're songs that sparked a relationship with science, with technology. I don't know if they sparked it, because I'd already done "Lunik 9" before. In any event, I already had a certain interest in science, speculation, new technology. But it got stronger when I got out of jail and beyond. To this day, right?

This prison experience – beyond the guitar
and the songs you wrote there – it led
you to discover yoga and macrobiotics. It
transformed your way of looking at the
world, your way of perceiving it. We can see it

in the songs that came after. I'd like to talk a little about your relationship with spirituality which characterizes some songs. Not necessarily songs that talk about religion.

This issue of spirituality was very pronounced in my work, indeed. "Tempo Rei," so many of my songs. To this day. Songs like "Prece," for example, from the last album. This one has more overt references to Catholic institutional religiosity, and to this thing of the search, the doubt, the unknown, the endless end of everything. I think that moment was fundamental because I reflected a lot on these issues. I remember one day I asked Sandra, who was my girlfriend at the time, who then became my wife, to bring me a yoga book. She brought me a yoga book and there I started to practice some asanas, the poses, and to understand what meditation was. I was starting to try certain meditation practices.

She also brought me a book, whose title was *Macrobiótica Zen*. She only started to be able to visit me on weekends after I'd been imprisoned for almost a month. I told her I'd read in a magazine – I think it was the magazine *O Cruzeiro* or *Manchete*, one of those – where John Lennon and Yoko were at one of those places in Amsterdam with the prostitutes in shop windows. Do you know those places? They're very interesting. And they decided to do what they called a bed-in. They spent about 15 days, more or less, on public display in one of those shop windows. And the reporters for *Manchete* or *O Cruzeiro* said that one of the interesting things about their intervention there was a food system that they started to adopt, which was macrobiotics. It was a system from Japan, from a master named George Oshawa.

All that stayed with me. Macrobiotic, food system, John Lennon. John Lennon's into it? Then there must be something to whatever this guy is inventing. So I asked Sandra to bring me a book, to find out if there were any macrobiotics books. She found one that had been published by the Associação Macrobiótica of Porto Alegre, in Rio Grande do Sul, a few months earlier. It was called *Macrobiótica Zen* and it explained the system, chewing, rice, cereals, soy, all that, soy sauce, miso. The Japanese thing, right?

Of course, there was no way I could adopt that in prison, but one day I called the official responsible for food, for the provision of food, and I told him: "Look, I'd like you to not give me meat. Give me beans, but give me some oats or something." Anyway, stuff like that. I asked him to fix something where I could start mimicking a macrobiotic diet. And it was no sooner said than done. When I got out of prison, I went to Salvador to make a record with Rogério Duprat. I called Duprat in São Paulo and told him: "Listen, bring me the key macrobiotic ingredients. Go to

Arroz de Ouro in Largo do Arouche, buy some things, and bring them." He brought me brown rice, all that stuff, and I started doing macrobiotics properly in Salvador.

It was in prison that these two things, yoga and macrobiotics, came into my life. I remember it was a transformation, from a physical point of view. Caetano always referred to this, he'd say: "Gil was one person before macrobiotics, and he became a different one afterwards."

**And do you think you became
a different composer too?**

I'm not sure... No, because the mystery of music and the enchanted presence of musical inspiration were already there and they remained with me. But if you take a record like *Quanta*, for example, you see a concentrated interest in science, in art, in the interrelationships between art and science, etc., right? All in a condensed work, like the album *Quanta*, 25 songs.

Many references, right?

Many references. To Candomblé, to this entire animated world, in other words, the relationship between the world of the soul, the anima, and the world of techne, of science and all that. So, without a doubt, that moment of prison inaugurated, let's say, it initiated all these things.

It's interesting that the songs you recorded during this period, within the traumatic experience of both prison and exile, are not depressing songs, right? On the contrary, "Aquele Abraço" is a song that refers to this release from prison, it's almost a celebration.

It was Ash Wednesday on the day we left the barracks in Realengo to go to the Federal Police downtown. I remember passing by Avenida Rio Branco, with all the carnival decorations still hanging on the walls. And then the words came: "Rio de Janeiro is still beautiful / Rio de Janeiro is still being." This song is directly based on that, because I mention my departure, I mention seeing the remnants of carnival on Rio Branco and Getúlio Vargas.

But the expression "aquele abraço" ("that hug") was one I heard often in the barracks from the soldiers, among themselves, constantly coming and going: "that hug, that hug." I thought: "But what is that hug? Where does this thing come from?" One day I asked one of them, I asked a soldier: "Why do you greet your colleagues with 'that hug'?" He said: "Oh, that's a famous catchphrase from a television show with Lilico," who was a very successful comedian. He had a television program whose catchphrase was "that hug."

I kept thinking about that. I even started greeting some soldiers in prison that way: "Hey, that hug." When I left on Ash Wednesday, I saw all that. And when I was on my way to Bahia after going to the Federal Police, on the plane I started writing the song. I finished it in Salvador.

**You then write another song about exile
when you return, "Back in Bahia."**

"As if going was necessary to come back / much more alive with a more lived life, half there and half here." [Brazilian counterculture icon] Rita Lee loves it, she says, "Only you [could come up with] 'A more lived life, half there and half here.' You're kind of crazy." I say: "I am."

**And the way you deal with spirituality
and the question of existence, of cycles, of
prison and exile. In 1976, you were arrested
for possession of marijuana. And there's a
fantastic scene in the documentary about Os
Doces Bárbaros, from the trial, where you**

Yes, my testimony in front of the judge. I said: "Look, marijuana, for example, or the LSD that I did in London, they were substances that helped me with introspection, you know?" Which leads to this whole field of speculation about transcendence, the spirit, what comes after, how it is, what we are, body, soul, all those things. And a lot of this through music too, because there's something about marijuana that activates something internally, in so-called verbal consciousness, mainly in the form of verbalization.

At least for me it was like that. It was a way to enable more peaceful walks through the field of music, harmony, melody, rhythm... It's not for nothing that reggae is the way it is. And bossa nova too. Because João Gilberto, everyone knows, was an appreciator. Without a doubt, there would be no bossa nova without marijuana. A heart and mind that have yielded to the generous properties of cannabinol can understand... it sparked so many things. João's concentration, his gentleness... Bob Marley's controlled intensity. All that. Without a doubt, marijuana played a huge role in all of this.

So, at that trial in front of the judge, I said this: "Look, for me it's recreational, of course, that's one thing. But it's much more, because I discovered in it a form of transportation to this field of introspection, this more interiorized field of meditation. Meaning, it helps me understand what is, why one meditates, what one meditates for." I got the impression that the judge understood. He was understanding. He was. He understood that it wasn't a prank. I used it carefully, I used it with such care, so that I would notice the benefits to me, as well as the harm. I stopped smoking because of an accelerated heart rate. At a certain point, cannabinol triggered a very strong tachycardia and I stopped smoking because of that when I was about 50 years old.

It might be hard to distinguish, but are there any songs of yours that are specifically dedicated to this kind of feeling? Any of your songs that have been especially influenced by the effect of marijuana or LSD?

I don't remember. Several were. Everything I just said here allows us to understand that my music has a lot of this influence. What's more, I had the audacity to attribute other musical breakthroughs to it as well. I mentioned João Gilberto here, right? I mean, it's not a joke, it's serious stuff. Marijuana is serious business. One thing that sustained me, let's say, in this position that I'm sharing here, that I'm articulating here in relation to drugs, but I'm sticking

to marijuana, because it was the one I most related to...
what made me discover, or let's say, what made me covet
this serious, scientific, religious aspect of marijuana was
Timothy Leary's book *The Politics of Ecstasy*, which I read
in London at the time. It's a book where he takes a broad
view. It begins with the LSD thing, because he was one of
the big ones, the first big champion of LSD consumption.
The guys from Sandoz in Switzerland sent him a sample,
and that's where he started, and he distributed it among
the university students, his students. And this book of his
provided a very well-done analysis of the various drugs.
He would start with LSD, then he would talk about marijuana, he would go on to drugs that he rejected, in short,
that he considered as threatening and destructive, in the
case of cocaine, heroin, etc. Reading Timothy Leary gave
me material to defend an argument like the one I made in
front of the judge in Florianópolis.

**The point is that this discussion and the
entire path your generation has taken in
relation to drugs faces a challenge nowadays
with the moralistic questions that are injected
into the debate.**

There are moral questions and there are social questions.
Criminalization, the whole problem of the marginalization

of a huge number of young people because of criminalization, all the harms arising, not from the substance, but from
its criminalization. All this has not erased or prevented us
from understanding the importance of that substance for the
medicinal world, and for the recreational world too. There's
a clearer understanding of the mind and the benefits.

***But don't you think a government with
a more conservative bias in moral terms
obstructs or hinders discussions like this and
others like it?***

Look, what I think is this: these dinosaurs, these conservatives who are proud to call themselves dinosaurs,
they will be destroyed by natural advances. They don't
have... Anyone who insists on taking a stand against history, against desire, against discovery, invention, human
research, the development of contemporary man, cannot
help but lose out to natural advances... We have to worry
about them now, as long as they're out there trying to mess
with our lives. But in terms of the future, in terms of natural
progression, the law of accelerated returns that Kurzweil
and so many other scientists talk about... The returns are
accelerating, the returns provided by science, by introspection. The unity that is being achieved between science and
religion in the quantum world, the discovery of quantum

mechanics, the uncertainty principle with the discovery that the particles, microparticles, the smallest particles of matter exist and do not exist at the same time, it depends on how we position ourselves... Our life, therefore, is this: permanent creation beginning with ourselves. I think all these things are irreversible, they are there because they tend toward that. This is all quantum mechanics, it's all modern science, it's Einstein, it's Planck, it's Heisenberg. That's it.

Take the photoelectric cells that open the doors before we get to them with that profound exactitude, such that we're no longer afraid of them not opening. In the past we worried, "Will they open?" Now we don't. We come and go and we know they will open automatically... This automatism is made possible by the micro-dimension of matter. In any case, it's no use for conservatives and reactionaries to try to fight this, because it's not possible. The entire economy, all the progress, right? In transportation, in medicine, whatever field you imagine, they depend on this ever-greater progressive encounter between science, religions, customs, manners, openness, freedom, respect for others, all that. So, it's no use being against it. Go against it, so what?

But there are issues like the Amazon, for example.

Yes, but that's just it. That's a good example. What does the Amazon inspire in the world today? For scientists, for responsible politicians, for responsible young activists, what does it inspire? It inspires responsibility, the notion of care, the notion of belonging. We all belong to nature. Alongside the technological advances that will lead us to the supercomputer and artificial intelligence that will surpass the brain within 50 years at most, alongside all this, there is nature, the knowledge of the Indigenous peoples, of natural peoples, which must be preserved.

Everyone knows that, that's what the Amazon is today. You can't just burn the land to open a field for soybeans or whatever else. You can see that the people who are more opposed to the Brazilian government's retrograde positions right now are agribusiness. Why? Because they're following these developments, those who are truly interested and attentive. They know things are moving towards the future. Before long, the question of meat, cattle, beef... before long, artificial meat will be here. There are already many many new biotechnology projects.

Oil will run out; it will be replaced by new forms of energy. It's already there, you already have it today. You go to Austria, you see the new windmills catching the air to produce wind energy. You see solar energy cells. So, it's no use for these people to sit there and say we have to go back to the 18th century, to the 17th century. We won't.

The arrow of time points forward, it doesn't go backwards. Nobody goes back to the past. But everyone has the possibility to move into the future.

So that's how it is. The future is, on the triad, on the axis of the equation present-past-future, it is what determines advancement, knowledge, openness, the permanent doubt that nourishes science. So that's it. I'm not worried about these people.

We are getting near the end, but first I wanted you to talk about one of the songs you composed this century, which is one of your most striking, "Não Tenho Medo da Morte" (I'm Not Afraid of Death). How did you write it?

I was in a meeting. I was Minister of Culture at the time, and I went to a meeting in Seville, Spain, with various thinkers and scientists – António Damásio, who is a very important neuroscientist, John Perry Barlow, who died recently – and there was a discussion about what we just talked about here, the advances in techne, the great discoveries about the brain, brain plasticity, and all that stuff, neuroscience, biotechnology. It was a meeting about all these fields. And the question of man's longevity, survival, or even eternal permanence in a state of life, that was one of the themes, one of the things that for three days we debated and talked about.

When I arrived at the hotel one night after the day's meetings, I sat down, Flora went to bed. I was at the little table in the living room, and then this poem came to me. It came to me already complete, and in half an hour I'd written down the whole thing. When I got back to Brazil, I called my son Bem and told him: "Look, there's something here that I want you to help me write a song for." So, he programmed it on the computer, and I started singing, making it up on the spot. Later I made this version, which is more elaborated:

"I'm not afraid of death / But I'm afraid of dying / What's the difference / You have to ask / It's that Death is after / When I stop breathing / Dying is still here / In life, in the sun, in the air / There may still be pain / Or the desire to piss / Death is after / There won't be anyone / Like me here now / Thinking about the beyond / There will no longer be a beyond / The beyond will be a then / I'll have neither feet nor head / Neither liver nor lung / How will I be afraid / If I don't have a heart? / I'm not afraid of death / But I'm afraid of dying, yes / Death and the after-me / But I'm the one who's going to die / My last act / And I'll have to be present / Just like a president / Swearing in the successor / I'll have to die living / Knowing that I'm going / So in that instant, yes / I'll suffer perhaps a shock / A stroke or a thud / A shiver or a touch / Natural things of life / Just like eating, walking / Dying from a killed death / Dying from a died death / Maybe I'll miss you / As with any farewell."

INTERVIEW 2: CONDUCTED REMOTELY BY ANA PAULA SIMONACI, LEONARDO LICHOTE, PAULO ALMEIDA AND SERGIO COHN IN OCTOBER 2020

Gil, how is daily life with social distancing, due to the pandemic? Have you been able to maintain a routine? Or have the days been freer? How have your days been?

Ah, it's a process of gradual adaptation to the demands of the current situation – social distancing chief among them, which is taxing for many, but not so much for me. I adapt well to isolation, to being more removed from social life. But then there's the issue of taking precautions, following public health measures, the issue of discipline in this sense, of always washing your hands when you get home after going out to go to the dentist or to have a COVID test. In short, there's this apparatus of living with the threat of contamination. That was one very important issue. The other was how to spend your time at home. I've read eleven books since May. I traveled twice, I left Copacabana to go to Araras three times, mainly in June, when I did a French TV show in Araras and then the São João livestream on my birthday.

The early days, from a psychological point of view, were very difficult. The first two months. Because it coincided with the deaths in Italy and Spain, which caused a lot of fear. Soon thereafter it arrived in Brazil and the United States. And with all the agony around the hospitalized, the old folks, with the issue of oxygen, that whole thing, that hospital side of the pandemic was very agonizing for the first two months. Later, we got accustomed to it.

And I'd said that the isolation itself, the fact of being isolated itself, wasn't a major difficulty for me, because I'm already very reclusive. I've been living these past few years at home anyway, except when I'm forced to travel abroad to play shows. I stay at home a lot, I'm very much a homebody. So, I'm already used to this issue of managing my own schedule – what time I watch television, what time I read, what time I play the guitar. All these things were already on my map.

And is this the right routine?
Do you have time to wake up, exercise, eat?

Generally, I do a yoga workout with [my wife] Flora and do some light strengthening exercises in the middle of the day. Things like that. The time is very open, right? The separation between day and night becomes less clear. Because you don't have to work outside the house during the day or at night, so everything is kind of fluid. There were periods when I stayed up until 3, 4, 5 in the morning reading in bed, after having spent two to three hours watching television. I watched TV a lot during news hours, mainly watching longform news shows between 6pm and midnight. I watched a lot of television at those hours and then after midnight I would read. I read until late.

During the day I played the guitar. In the afternoon, I'd basically play the guitar and improvise a lot. I didn't really want to compose songs and I didn't dedicate myself to composing practically anything, but I kept improvising harmonic series and things like that.

You said you read a lot. What
have you read during this period?
And what interested you the most?

I read mostly science. I read more books about astronomy, about physics, chemistry, quantum physics. I read about the experiments of German science during Nazism. The construction of the atomic bomb, the war after the first arrival of the atomic bomb. The German projects, the British and American projects. It's something I've been researching for a long time. I have this great interest in science and technology. So, it was an opportunity to take a little deeper dive into these themes.

We just published a book by Mário Schenberg, who was an important physicist and an art critic, and a close friend of yours. It's an essay called "Art and Technology."

How interesting! Mário Schenberg played a very important role in my album *Quanta*. The first promotion I did for the album was actually a lecture at [the public university] Unicamp where he lived after retirement. He connected me with the university. I gave a very interesting lecture, precisely about art and science. *Quanta* opens with a song called "Ciência e Arte" by Cartola and Carlos Cachaça, which was a samba for a Mangueira parade in the 1950s. Right at the beginning of the decade, 1951, 1952… And the samba talks about [20th century physicist] César Lattes and all that stuff. So Mário was very important during the period I was writing the album.

And before that, actually. Jorge Mautner introduced him to me when I was doing *Dia Dorim Noite Neon*, which had a preview of what would become *Quanta*. And I visited Mário two or three times at his house. We talked a lot. In addition to the scientific interest, there was the whole issue of his political-ideological involvement. He was the one who asked me to write a song for South Africa, at that crucial moment in the anti-apartheid struggle: "Oração Pela Libertação da África do Sul" (Prayer for the Liberation of South Africa). Mário discussed all those relations between Brazilian Indians, African Indians, Afro-Brazilian indigeneity, all that stuff, these general concerns. Mário was very important to me. He was one of Jorge Mautner's intellectual mentors. He was an artist who was very close to me and who was willing to share everything, ideas, music, thoughts about life, about the world, about philosophy, about all of that.

Your interest in science and technology has followed you since the 1960s. On your first album, there's the track "Lunik 9", then "Cérebro Eletrônico," and so on. It's a concern that has stayed with you in your music as well.

Exactly. Because it was a residual childhood interest that emerged during the war. I was born in 1942, in the middle of [World War II], at the height of the confrontation between the Allies and Nazism. My father followed all this with great interest, especially the issues of the battlefield, the confrontation between armies and armaments. And my father subscribed to two magazines specialized on the war, on the weapons, destroyers, submarines, fighter planes, tanks. And starting from the height of the war, I spent time leafing through those magazines, enchanted by all those things, those weapons.

Then, right after that, there was the question of the bomb in Japan, the atomic bombs and all that. So when I reached adolescence and pre-adulthood, having developed interests in other areas, including music, I went back to pondering what I called the residue of childhood. This residue of interest in technology and science took hold right away. So much so that when Sputnik was launched, I was already thinking about it. When [the Russian spacecraft] Lunik became the first craft to actually go to the moon, I wrote the song "Lunik 9," combining a certain romantic vision about moonlight, about the past, about the moon's role in human subjectivity; combining that with science, with the rocket that had taken that craft to the moon.

And that was the first blossoming of this scientific interest in song, right? It was later joined by "Cérebro Eletrônico" in prison, and the other one I also wrote in prison, "Futurível."

Another interesting aspect of Mário Schenberg which is similar to what I see in you too, is the bringing together of Eastern and Western thought, right? He has science, but does he have Zen? Did you talk to him about it?

Yes. Very much. About the Vedas and the full force of Indian philosophy and the great esoteric societies with sources in India and branches across Europe. Nazism itself, in fact, has a fundamental basis in this question of the Thule Society, which was an initiatory society, a secret society. It influenced not only Hitler, but the entire core group of the Nazi Party. So, all these things, we talked a lot about all this.

How do you see war? Your temperament is a peaceful one. The impression we have of you is of a peaceful being. And war, you say that it emerges as a childhood interest that connects to the thirst for knowledge. Many peaceful people recognize the importance of war, or the dynamics of war or the way war is intrinsically human and how it objectively advances technology. It proposes technological advances that are used later, often to improve the quality of life of populations. I wanted you to talk a little about your perspective on war based on this fascination that comes from childhood.

War is brutality, a beast, isn't it? The wild beast that inhabits the human being and manifests itself periodically, through this discharge of accumulated brutalist energy. That's what war is. Historically, it's one of the main forms of human action, of human society – territorial conquest, conquest of strategic materials in other distant territories... And, as you said, all this comes alongside the natural propulsion of technique, of techne, of the use of artifacts of all kinds. Artifacts and mind-facts [*artefatos e mentefatos*]. All war has this function, so we cannot ignore it.

We must consider the fact that war has been one of the main sources of creative energy discharge in all human societies to date. Creative energy for destruction, creating to destroy. And this whole thing is fascinating from the perspective of the play of opposites. Within balance is the equal possibility of the extremes. So, war is an extreme to which humanity always resorts and, on the other side, pacifists all resort to all these other forms of appeasement of the human mind, of the human heart. So, it's natural, war and peace. "Only war makes our love in peace."

And you said you're not composing. You haven't composed anything recently?

I composed a song for Andrucha Waddington's TV series, *Sob Pressão*, which takes place in a hospital. A song with Ruy Guerra. It was the soundtrack for these last two episodes of *Sob Pressão* which deals precisely with COVID, right? And it was the only song I wrote. Ruy Guerra and I wrote the lyrics, and I wrote the music. And Chico Buarque recorded it with me, because he was the one Andrucha commissioned. Andrucha commissioned Chico to write the music with Ruy Guerra. Andrucha wanted to involve Ruy and Chico in the composition, but Chico ruled it out, and said: "Talk to Gil. Tell Ruy to discuss this matter with Gil. I'll record the song after it's done." That's what he did.

One more thing about science: how do you see the issue of the attack on science these days?The way people are relativizing scientific knowledge, a certain obscurantism has been emerging. Have you been following this?

It's all a flash in the pan. Science has already dominated the direction of human destiny. There is no future without science. It's impossible. All the enjoyment it's possible to obtain today from modern life, everything comes from science. Even this thing we're doing right now, this enjoyment we're getting from images from a distance, in short, from this new method of communication that the internet has created. All this is science, all this comes exactly from the great scientific discoveries of the late nineteenth century, early twentieth century. Relativity, quantum mechanics, all that stuff.

How are you going to discard all that now? These advances? Everything, knowledge about stars, about galaxies. Nanotechnology, biotechnology. How are you going to discard these things? There's no way. Science, medicine, all the human forms of caring for man himself, all of them benefit from science, from techniques. It's impossible to get rid of science. Obscurantism is a brutalist reaction against the Enlightenment sensibility that science affords. But science has already won.

The question now is how to provide science with mechanisms for its own regulation, for its own domestication, for its own possibility of progress toward the future without terrible accidents. This is the question: how to avoid possible accidents. How to avoid bombs.

If science has already asserted itself in the long-run, in the short-run obscurantism still gets some victories though, doesn't it?

8. In 2019, newly elected President Jair Bolsonaro abolished the Ministry of Culture and merged some of its functions into a newly created "Ministry of Citizenship."

But that's what I said before. This provisional condition of adopting violence as a form of persuasion, as a form of human subordination... this is the old logic of warlords, understand? Economic, cultural, and properly military war. All these things. These wars are built to disguise the fact that we are already in the grip of a technological development that advances, advances, advances, and will continue to advance. And there's no way around it anymore.

And the issue of institutions in Brazil today? The dismantling of institutions that is taking place, like the end of the Ministry of Culture?[8] How do you see this issue?

That's even more provisional than what we were just talking about. It's part of a simple process of substituting the elite in power. In other words, the very wheel of democracy takes care of that by alternating those in power. This cannot last. This will last as long as it seems to contribute to the development of human society. The moment it becomes clearly understood that this is the opposite – that it is obscurantism, regression – then the mentality of progressive rationality again takes over. It assumes its place once again. So, it's all very provisional. Having the extreme right in power is a passing thing.

No, no. It's like we talked about. It reflects a certain tranquility on my part in relation to all this. I mean, the play of opposites is natural. So, you're here at one extreme one moment, and at the other extreme the next. This leads to the search for the intermediate, the middle path. Find the middle way in all the fields of your life. The middle path becomes the place where things flow naturally, where it all empties out. And all of this is informed by a basic principle, which is that of mortality, of finitude. In other words, every human effort is aimed at neutralizing this possibility of finitude. And that always implies that "it's the future that matters." It's up ahead that matters. It's the improvement of the human condition that matters, the preparation of the human condition for occupying the universe which is primary, the great desire, the great purpose of intelligence. Anyway, that's it.

*[Brazilian musician] Jorge Mautner always
quotes that phrase of Sartre's, that what*

*matters to man is the conquest of death and
the conquest of the stars.*

Yes, that's it. Through the increasingly clear advances of science, technique, mastery, rationality. The arrival of the computer, for example, is an auspicious development in the world. Everything that cyberspace has brought, the great achievements of electronics. The issue is that scientists are quiet. They work quietly. They work in silence, in part to avoid the possibility of manipulation by the warlords. So, scientists are careful. They are dedicated, profoundly dedicated.

For instance, with this pandemic – to give a somewhat superficial example of the profoundness associated with the man of science, the man of technique – the doctors and researchers are working quietly to find the cure, to find the vaccine, to find the most complete knowledge about the virus, about how it progresses. This conversation between scientists and the virus – this "friendly" dialogue, I'd even call it – this way of considering the virus an ally for one's own enlightenment, for the enlightenment of the mind, the heart, for knowledge, this is the role of the scientist. This is the role of the man of science. He does his work and he leaves aside these immediate ambitions of the warlords, the obscurantists. What the scientist is concerned with is this – he knows he's subject to finitude here, but he seeks infinity up ahead. That's what he's dedicated to.

And the artist?

The same thing. Science is art.

The way you approach family lineage is a way to conquer death, right? Because you play with ancestry, both forward and backward. For example, I see you just released an EP with your granddaughter Flor, that's a continuation. Or the collaborations with [your son] Bem Gil...

That's it. This is the function of procreation, isn't it? This is the function of extending ourselves and our individualities through our children. Through the production of everything, including the production of the biological. Reproduction plays a very important role in all of this. So, when our children appear, when our grandchildren appear, what happens in our hearts is a kind of coronation of everything. We feel we've been crowned.

That's where death starts to appear peaceful, where extinction becomes a more peaceful thing. These things that seem to some degree unbearable are put into perspective. Your son is over there doing things, your grandson is over there doing things, the grandchildren of so many others, the great-grandchildren and everything else. If you see the process of procreation at work, you feel more relaxed. You know that, "There. There's meaning in my having been here." In being here as long as necessary, as long as life allows. The work of extending life's duration – a task with which science is concerned, with which knowledge is concerned, the traditional knowledge of the plant from the Indian in the forest, whose dreams showed what was good for healing this or that – all these things, this knowledge from various sources, it's all reassuring. Okay, we know that we're here doing what we need to do, all of us. And when life says it's over, it's over. Because life will continue in everything, consciousness will migrate to other configurations.

And the micro-micro-micro-particles of everything will also come together in other ways, in other configurations, in other densities, right? As I say in the song "Futurível": "You were called, you will be transmuted into energy / Your second humanoid stage begins today / Stay calm, let's begin the transmission / My system will change / Your dimension / Your body will transform / Into lightning, it will transport itself / In space, it will recover / Many light-years beyond / Beyond / The new cohesion / It will give you a mortal heart again // The new movement may seem strange to you / Yours eyes may be copper, your arms tin / Don't worry, my system will maintain / The awareness of being / You will think / Your body will be brighter / The mind, smarter / Everything in super dimension / The mutant is happier / Happy because / In the new mutation / Happiness is made of metal."

That's it. I'm saying, you can be reconfigured. This dimension that is here now, with everything seemingly under its absolute control, this physical condition, this must disappear at a certain moment to give way to another configuration.

But this tranquility, this reassurance that comes with the presence of children and grandchildren, this feeling of "mission accomplished" that you're talking about – doesn't it cool down the desire to create, the desire to continue creating? What drives the artist to carry on?

It purifies. It distills the creator instinct, the creative instinct. It shapes this instinct into a form that is more suited to this new mentality, to the way your mind, feelings, and thoughts are currently configured. It's the opposite of a cooling, it's a purification of the creative vein. It's really a distillation. You transform quantity into quality. That's what it is, in the same way a gram of uranium can be transformed into an immensity of electrons, in short, into energy. That's the way the atomic bomb is, that's the way all these other things are. The small becomes big, the smaller gets bigger. Doing fewer things with more density, with more intensity, purifies the creative and creator instinct.

I was just thinking that there's one thing in your music that's very clear: it's a space for thought. Many times there's a thesis, an idea being put forward. When did you realize that music was not just a space for that concept of beauty, or melody, or love, or feeling, but a space or a vehicle for thought, for transmitting ideas? For constructing an almost philosophical or metaphysical thought through music?

It was when I started to understand that music was a form of expression for myself, for all my complexity. Music could be an outlet for diverse flows, for diverse fluxes of thought and feeling and understanding and misunderstanding. In short, for mystery. A space to talk about mystery, the unattainable, the agony that invades us when we cannot reach an understanding of something, when we cannot achieve tolerance, when we can't achieve forgiveness, when we can't achieve those things that are essential for self-actualization.

So from there, in the course of making songs and doing music you discover that you can talk about everything. Not only can you; you must talk about everything. A song must be an instrument for this, for manifesting the general complexity that inhabits you and that, consequently, since you are similar to others, inhabits everyone else. And there is the need to communicate to others your own discoveries – your own major doubts, your major feelings like love, in its various forms.

All of this becomes a basic ingredient in songwriting, so you're no longer stuck making romantic love songs. You don't need to be stuck with anything. A song about mystery can be a great expression or declaration of love for a person, or for thousands or millions of people. You're there, subject to the entirety of what you are, to your whole being, in all its forms coming from every side.

In order to understand the composer within this complex whole, it seems to me that there are two "awakenings" that are fundamental:

*sex and death. How did you see this in your
life?*

You said sexual awakening. The silence of sex is another awakening. It precedes that of finitude, in the case of mature human beings. It must be a necessary awakening prior to awakening to finitude. Silencing sex, because what is sex? Sex is the great mechanism of creation, of reproduction. It is the lust for multiplying oneself, the lust for being in others, for being you yourself in other unfolded bodies. This flow is the basis for the profound consciousness that is sex. Profound sex is that. So, there comes a time when this whole thing of "mission accomplished" – making peace with things, orders, and goals achieved – there comes a time when sex is silence.

*And this can all be very powerful.
And very scary as well. Both the
awakening of sex and the
awakening of the silence of sex...*

Exactly. This is frightening for me, as it is for everyone else. Frightening, but at the same time there's a feeling of "what an extraordinary manifestation!" What a confirmation, what an extraordinary affirmation that sex is for our being, for our human condition, for our individuality, even.

That's what sex is – it's an affirmation of individuality, isn't it? In other words, reproduction needs individuation to join with individuation so that there is a continuation of that pleasure of living that sex carries. All that was my discovery of sex. Obviously, in those initial moments when this thing appeared, there wasn't this degree of conscious elaboration around what sex was. All that was an extraordinary surprise and it brought threats at the same time, right? There was the great explosion of pleasure, but at the same time the threats and the suspicion that it could be exhausted. At a certain point, that form of transforming life into energy must be exhausted so that other forms of energy might be reserved for the future.

All that was present in those first moments of sexual life. But everything was leading to what I said. At some point, this explosion of the sexual lexicon comes to the disappearance of words about it. Silence. The disappearance of the grammar of sex. Verbs, nouns, adjectives, descriptors of sex are no longer needed. The verbalization of sex and all these things disappear, giving way to something else. Out there at the ends of the universe, what will the question of sexuality be like? Will it exist?

Death has been a theme of yours since you were young, with "Ele Falava Nisso Todo Dia" and other songs.

"Death is queen that reigns alone / It does not need our call / Fear / To arrive" ("Death").

Meanwhile with sex, which songs do you feel carry this energy the most? "Sonho Molhado" ("Weat Dream")?

"Sonho Molhado" is a big joke about it, right? But look, I don't even know. I'd have to review the whole repertoire to figure it out, but there are many. Some songs are more directly linked to people, figures, women who energetically magnetized me. Not just women, but men too. There's this whole thing of the languages through which sexuality expresses itself. I choose the smoother, more ethereal ways of expressing what people expect to see more crudely. The brutalism of sexuality. So, I always chose these milder forms, the more ethereal sayings, flavors, and softer scents.

You talked about songs for women and for men too. Was any song made directly for a man in that sense?

In the sense of sexual impact, no. But I have several about the profound affective impact of men. There's "Pai e Mãe." There's "Ele e Eu," which is a song I wrote for Caetano, the one on the record *Expresso 2222*. There are several.

Listen, I'm not sure how to answer that question. Firstly, because there's been this downsizing within myself that I already referred to here. The drying of this creative instinct, which no longer requires the presence of these very refined substances in my own creation, these very deep, deeply explicit understandings of time, of eternity, of all these things.

And also I don't really mine these dimensions from other works, from other creators. For example, nowadays with rap. Rap has such an absolute plethora of semantics and trans-semantics, lexicons and trans-lexicons involved in its creation, I don't even go fishing there anymore. You take a rap like that, one of the best out there, they're saying so many things at the same time, right? And at the same time, they're not saying anything, they're just trying to throw you forward, to throw you into that moment where you throw yourself off the hill and the hang-glider supports you with the force of the air. You want to be held up by the air now.

That's what rap is. It's music that wants… it's the senses, the addresses, the messages, it's all there. Except in some more obvious cases, where you have the right instrumentation for ideological transmission, for political transmission, etc. But, in general, the great works, the great songs these days are like this – they're hang-glider flights over the general panorama of reality below. I no longer think: "What is this kid trying to say? What is that girl trying to sing?" In short, it's all of that. The vocals were already so refined, the young people are all outfitted with so much technology, with so many tools, with so many instruments to do things from the point of view of words, sounds, and everything, that I'm not very concerned about mining the semantic nuggets.

And how do you listen to music these days?

One of the ways I listen to music lately is to try to play songs as much as possible through my guitar. Maybe a samba by Walter Santos. "How can I reproduce this on the guitar?" An old samba by Walter Santos, when he was still with João Gilberto, with impressionistic elements from Juazeiro in Bahia. It's that kind of thing. It's taking an old samba by Batatinha and trying to play that on the guitar, trying to solo on that, something I've never managed before. Or a Jobim theme, or a Van Halen riff. Playing a Van Halen riff on a guitar. "How did he do that? How could he do that? Let's see." Or a melodic phrase by Paul McCartney, in one of his songs. Or being deeply enchanted by a song by Luiz Gonzaga.

For example, when I did my birthday party with songs from the Northeastern repertoire, in the style of a *festa junina*, it gave me enormous pleasure. It was pure orgasm, you know? Singing: "In Rio everything's changed / On the nights of São João / Instead of polka and rancheira / People just dance and ask for baião / In the middle of the street / It's a balloon / It's a bonfire / It's a fire / But on the dance floor / People just dance and ask for baião / Oh, oh, oh, oh, São João / Oh, oh, oh, oh, São João." Shouting that "Oh, oh, oh, oh, São João" is like a sexual climax.

These songs came to me at a time when energy was building up in an extraordinary way in my body, in my being, in my mind, in everything else. So when I'm able to go back to them today and turn these expressions into something new, it's a huge pleasure. And that's my relationship with music today. It is a purified relationship that comes in sudden fragments of things I heard in my childhood, in my youth, which manifest themselves and come with enormous grandeur. So, I'm not really worried about which record to listen to anymore. Not at all. Just the memory of one of Jimi Hendrix's riffs is enough.

**2020 was marked by Black Lives Matter and
the racial issue in Brazil and in the world.
How do you see it in your personal trajectory?
When did the awareness of racial struggle
awaken in you?**

I don't even think it was a moment, but rather a succession of several fragments of moments. Why? Because this issue was not an issue in the early part of my life. This question did not arise in my childhood. Because I came from a family where my father was a *mestiço* Black man. My mother was a *mestiça* Black woman, even more so than him, because in her case the mixture with Indians was much more explicit than in his case. He was a lot more *afro-descendente* and she was more *india-descendente*. The family lived in a kind of middle-class elite bubble in a small town, a tiny country town, where they were extraordinarily respected figures. He was a doctor who tended to everyone, rich and poor, Blacks and whites, etc. Her as well. She was a school teacher. In small towns, communities were strongly self-referential, right? They referenced themselves. People mattered to each other. The blacksmith – the man who worked the iron and made the tools for the horse harness, etc. – was as important as the judge who worked in the courthouse. Or the parish priest who was in charge of the religious stuff. So, people had obvious value. People were worth a lot, all of them, whoever they were, Black, white, poor or middle class. The fireworks maker, Mr. Sinésio, a man who made fireworks for the Saint John's Day festivities – that man was something, he was of immense importance to us all.

So, the issue of these divisions, race, class, all these issues didn't come up. There was no room for them. These questions did not appear. Nobody was racist in that little town. It couldn't, just couldn't be, couldn't be. There was no way. Everyone was equal within a kind of affective equilibrium and within several other orders.

So, it was only gradually that I became aware of this. When I got to high school in the city of Salvador, that school was an important agglomeration of the children of the Bahian elite, of wealthy farmers from the interior who sent their children to study in Salvador, or of the urban elite of Salvador itself, with its famous liberal professionals, lawyers, doctors, engineers. Those families there were already subject to a certain scrutiny that involved racialization and social class.

Then these things started to appear, they started awakening differences. I started to be different, I started to diffe-
rentiate myself as an individual from then on. Until then,
until 10, 12 years old, I was no different from anyone else.
Nobody was different from me in any way. These feelings
only came into existence there later on. Obviously, I had to
take positions in relation to myself. What am I? Ah, I'm a
mestiço Black man. Ah, I have different skin, different hair
from the other. Different values were attributed to these
differences by society in general. Ah, so I'm worth more
or less than A or B or C. So, these things came into being
there. And then, yes, one becomes aware of the differences
and how one must operate within these differences. You
for yourself, and for others. Then the issue of class struggle
appears, the issue of racial struggle appears, all these things
appear, and then you take your positions as a result of this
and as a result of that.

**And was your visit to Africa, in the late 1970s,
very important in this regard?**

Very important in that regard, of course. You go there
and see your origins, the place all these things came from
– that way of being, that way of walking, that way of re-
lating to plants, to animals. Then you can see their origins
and the many differences between their origins and those

of others. But as you become aware of these differences, this coincides with the fact that you're looking for more harmonizing elements within your life. You go looking for knowledge, you go looking for yoga, you go looking for this, you go looking for that, you go looking for all these elements that equalize the differences.

So, you don't... I didn't get involved with any wars, any armed militancy, any of these movements, whether around race, class, or anything like that. I remained a relatively balanced person between these various poles. Anyway, that's why. And, at the same time, as much as possible, I honor the anti-racist fight, the fight for economic equality, for solidarity, for all these things. But at the same time, without needing to put myself out there as personally imbued with these needs, because I'm not.

As I said, I am the son of a middle-class family, of prestigious liberal professionals. My grandmother was even a teacher. In Salvador, she taught several figures who were important to the city's political, economic, and commercial life. She was a celebrated teacher, known as a great teacher. So, I wasn't exactly dogged by these issues from an individual point of view. I had to see all this within the broader social arena beyond my own experience, expressing solidarity with just fights and good struggles.

How do you see identitarian struggles today?

Particularized identities have many allies. There is less and less possibility of isolating identities in their own field of configuration. Look at the question of George Floyd, the Black man who was murdered by the police in the US, and from which the Black Lives Matter movement emerged. Most of the people in the streets of New York or London were white. Discussion over. They're already out there. The issue of skin color is over, it's been overcome. There's still a residue that exists and will last for a while among some stubborn segments that want to maintain a social difference through color. Those "pig spirits," to use a very popular expression, want to stay there, hold on to separatism, and the hegemony inherited from colonial life. The racists have already lost. It's over. It's the same thing when we were talking about science at the beginning of our conversation here. These things are being overcome naturally. "Ah, you mean without struggle?" No, it's through struggle, it's through the conflict itself. But in dialectics, in the permanent dialogue between conflicting positions. In this thing that is the middle way. The just middle contains the equal possibility of the extremes. More and more, we seek and manage to capture a sense of justice in the middle ground of things, the justice that is in the middle of everything. Increasingly. That's why, when it's time to be in favor of affirmative action, you have to be in favor of racial quotas, just like when it's time to be in favor of [all-Black cultural association] Ilê Aiyê barring whites from participating as members. Keeping both in play to enrich the argument, as much for one side as for the other. You admit a quota on one side to force the antiquota to improve its argument, and vice versa. And in this way, you'll find ever greater alliances between different camps.

That's how I feel, how I think. That's why I'm here on the side of fiery speech one moment, but the next I'm there, on the side of gentle speech.

Conversation, dialogue, seems to be a fundamental principle for you. Not only a political principle, but an existential one as well.

That's it.

Have you been able to keep the conversation going during this period? And who are your main interlocutors? Who were your main interlocutors in the big conversations in your life?

Ah, there are a lot of people, a lot of friends, a lot of colleagues, a lot of important people. We've already mentioned Jorge Mautner and Mário Schenberg, to give two examples of very important dialogues. All the great creators, the great literati of Brazilian literature, the great Andrades, Oswald and Mário. The great poets, actually. Dialogue is not necessarily something you have, that you set up in a tête-à-tête conversation or in a specific squabble between one, or two, or three people. Dialogue is this permanent cloud, this permanent movement from the evaporation of understanding and misunderstanding. This permanent vapor of understanding and misunderstanding feeds you, lubricating your ability to breathe, your ability to live. It's art, science, poetry, and action all together at the same time. So, as I've become more isolated and older, I don't have so many face-to-face dialogues. The interlocutions are more fragmented. And, at this moment in which we live, I'm here talking to you, for example, through a computer application. Something that wasn't possible ten, fifteen, twenty years ago.

During the period of this pandemic, in these four, five months, I participated in so many livestreams linked to everything, to political movements, scientific movements, artistic movements, this, that, and the other. A huge amount. There were days like that when I did four, five livestreams a day. Some with people from universities here, people from universities in America, people from political movements in Europe. Anyway, a thousand things. So the interlocution is open. The world of interlocution is very wide.

Oh, it's possible. Chances are, yes. Although I can't tell you one thing specifically. "Oh, I shouldn't have done this, shouldn't have done that." Everything I did was because I believed it was something to be considered. I don't regret anything. There's nothing I wouldn't have done. Maybe I would do it again with a different window dressing, with a different flair. But, in essence, my reasons for doing the things I did, the reasons are all still there.

*At that time, you very clearly defended
the way culture was moving forward. The
changes that technology brought to the
dynamics of culture, of authorship. And you
have a very close dialogue with Creative
Commons. This all seems to have passed.
Today, we have an issue that we didn't have
at that time, which is the issue of social
media. Social media have
psychological implications for*

individuals, and they have political implications. For example, the direct change as a result of an election. How do you see this issue of social media?

Social media and their various platforms. Just yesterday I was reading about the search in the United States, Europe, and elsewhere, for minimally effective regulation that would allow even the slightest domestication of these large companies. And the story was basically about Amazon, Google, Facebook. All those people there, everyone. The committees in US Congress, the committees in the European Union debating these issues, the legal framework of the internet in Brazil. All these questions are so important, and they weren't present yet during the romantic phase of our relationship with the technological innovations around the digital network. It was our honeymoon period with the internet. There weren't yet these major interests, these major developments in the sense of hegemonizing and monopolizing these platforms. Now there are. Now this thing presents itself. And so it's necessary to mobilize all the world societies around this, to think about what kind of regulation is necessary, and what kind of response we demand to the questions that are arising across the world about these things.

It's a critical phase now, a phase where capital has heavily entered the digital environment. The various capitalisms got into it bigtime. There is the capitalism of China, there is the capitalism of the West. All of them are producing things more and more rapidly in this field. So, individuals and collectives are being called to account, to respond, to seek answers from the big platforms.

At the same time, you have alongside all this, an even more regressive obscurantism that wants the wideness of the world, multiculturalism, globalization, all these things to disappear from the map. How? How is it possible to stop being a globalist? How? To stop being a 'worldist'? How? By closing our borders, by closing ourselves in at the borders? How?

*I remembered you talking about this
with [critical geographer] Milton Santos,
whom you interviewed in the 1990s, about
alternative globalisms. Do you think this is
still possible? Or do you think we will also
have to deal with a hegemonic globalism?*

No. There are several, increasingly fragmented globalisms. They fragment more and more. They increasingly move toward what I said, toward that vapor. They are increasingly nebulized in this great global cloud, with accumulations here and there, with a search for hegemony here and there. The issue of China today, for example. It's finished with communism. People keep talking about "communism" and "retrograde groups," always talking about communism. What communism? That's pure capitalism over there.

In general, the possibility of communization, of agglutination, of the conditions for more community-based interactions in human society, this is a natural consequence of all this development, of the spread of globalized life. Through providing necessary services to the poorest people, through the issue of refugees. They are all things at the same time now, as Arnaldo Antunes used to say. And there's not much of an alternative. People who want a more retrograde condition, who want to reach more fascist, Nazi depths, they may very well try, but they won't prevail.

Einstein talked about three bombs that worried him with respect to the future of humanity: the atomic bomb, the communications bomb, and the viral bomb. I wanted to know what you think about this moment we're living through with a pandemic. Will it be a historic moment?

I think it's significant, yes. It's important because, firstly, it's a complicated disease. The presence of a virus that is very new, very powerful, in a sense, very treacherous, has forced the world to a brutal standstill that no one thought would happen. Everything shut down, right? It paralyzed the movement of people, of human masses. It paralyzed the process of wealth production, work, economies, productivity, industries, trades. At the global level.

So I keep thinking, how are they going to deny globalization with a problem like this virus? The virus shows up and says: "Look, globalization, look at it. And I'm here, in the middle, disturbing you globally, all at once," forcing everyone to turn to their connections with one another. Science is there producing antidotes and vaccines as quickly as possible. Businesses are adapting. Industries, industrial production is adapting. Transport is adapting. Movement, forms of human movement are adapting. The virus bomb hit the aviation industry, for example. The bomb hit tourism, forcing us all to rethink all these issues, in all these fields.

So, the virus isn't irrelevant. The pathogen is very relevant.

The culture industry has also felt the impact.

In a major way. We are proof of this. The livestreams that were produced, the forms of survival that theater, cinema, music, had to find. This is all very relevant.

But, in economic terms, it's insufficient. Do you think the state should have given some kind of support, for example, to artists?

But it did. And not just here, everywhere in the world. The United States has dedicated nearly a trillion or more, a trillion and a half, to support various fields. Brazil came up with almost a trillion *reais*. 700 or 800 billion to address the various issues. Artists mobilized. The Aldir Blanc Law was enacted. The welfare state had to be reactivated in a major way. And that is there. The social welfare state has again assumed certain functions, certain roles in this whole thing. That's what I was saying, all capitalisms had to come together, get together. "Let's see how we can work together." They had to decapitalize themselves in a sense.

You have a recent song called "Prece" (Prayer). It sounds like a song that refers to actual spiritual practice. Do you pray?

Just today I prayed, a lot. I pray a lot.

And what do you pray for?

I ask this: that the righteous and the sinners understand each other, forgive each other, consider each other. That they give up whatever is necessary so the other can get closer. That I may create space, create an opening in my heart, create open spaces in my heart so that others from everywhere find shelter in it, in my heart. That I may open my heart. That's what prayer is all about. The prayer is for the heart to open so that it can fit everything it can in it. That's it. "My vagabond heart wants to hold the world within me." Isn't that it? That's it. One of Caetano's first songs, one of the deepest and most brilliant of all: "Coração Vagabundo."

It's an absolutely anti-colonialist way of thinking. Instead of conquering other people's spaces, bring the other into your space...

That's it. I mean, it's giving oneself, it's giving, in the sense of absolute mutualities. I open so that what's outside can occupy it, can come inside. And when what was outside arrives in here, my space becomes something else. It becomes made up of that which comes from outside as well. It obligates us to others within a generalized mutuality, to adapt to everyone. Everyone has a little of everyone else inside each one of us. That's it. It's "trans-individuation" isn't it? Everyone on one plane. That's what I want, I want humanity to be better. I want humanity to fulfill its purpose.

TIMELINE

1942	Gilberto Passos Gil Moreira is born in Salvador,
Bahia, on June 26, the first son of José Gil Moreira
(doctor) and Claudina Passos Gil Moreira (elementary
school teacher); after 20 days, the family returns
home to Ituaçu in the rural interior of the state.

1951	Gil moves to Salvador, where he lives
with his paternal aunt Margarida.

1952	Influenced by Luiz Gonzaga, whom he
listens to frequently on the radio, Gil
begins to learn the accordion.

1959	Plays accordion with the group Os Desafinados, an
instrumental ensemble that plays for birthday parties,
at schools, and in social clubs in Salvador. Gil plays with
the group until 1961, but also begins to play the guitar
thanks to the influence of João Gilberto and bossa nova.

1961	Studies business administration at the University of
Bahia, where he graduates in 1964.

1963	Records and releases his first album, *Gilberto Gil -
sua música, sua interpretação*, with four of his own
compositions; Gil is introduced to Caetano Veloso
by the producer Roberto Santana; shortly thereafter,
he also meets Maria Bethânia and Gal Costa.

1964	Gil, Caetano, Bethânia, Gal and Tom Zé
perform *Nós, por exemplo*, the inaugural
show at Teatro Vila Velha, in Salvador.

<table>
<tr><td>1965</td><td>Gil performs his first solo show, Inventário, directed by Caetano Veloso; Gil marries Belina and moves to São Paulo, where he begins working for Gessy-Lever; he performs alongside Caetano, Gal, Bethânia and Tom Zé in the show Arena canta Bahia, directed by Augusto Boal; Gil performs as a cast member in Augusto Boal's Tempo de guerra at the Teatro Oficina; he records the songs "Procissão" and "Roda" as singles.</td></tr>
<tr><td>1966</td><td>Nara de Aguiar Gil Moreira, the first daughter of Gil and Belina, is born; Gil obtains a record deal with Philips to record his first LP and leaves Gessy-Lever to devote himself entirely to music; Gil and his family move to Rio de Janeiro; Gil participates in the 1st Festival Internacional da Canção as a songwriter with "Minha senhora" (written with Torquato Neto and performed by Gal Costa) and the 2nd TV Record Festival de Música Popular Brasileira with "Ensaio geral" (performed by Elis Regina).</td></tr>
<tr><td>1967</td><td>Composes songs for the film Brasil ano 2000 by Walter Lima Jr.; Marília de Aguiar Gil Moreira, Gil and Belina's second daughter, is born; in March, Gil and Belina separate; Gil begins working with the manager Guilherme Araújo and in May he releases his first LP, Louvação; Gil begins living with Nana Caymmi, daughter of the songwriter Dorival Caymmi; Gil performs his song "Domingo no parque" accompanied by Os Mutantes in the 3rd TV Record Festival de Música Popular Brasileira and wins second place.</td></tr>
<tr><td>1968</td><td>Records the LP Tropicália ou panis et circensis with Caetano, Gal, Tom Zé, Nara Leão, Os Mutantes and</td></tr>
</table>

Rogério Duprat; he releases the tropicalist album *Gilberto Gil*; the song "Divino, maravilhoso" (written in partnership with Caetano and performed by Gal) wins third place in the 4th TV Record Festival; on December 27th, Gil and Caetano are arrested in São Paulo under the auspices of the Brazilian dictatorship's AI-5 decree.

1969 Released from prison, Gil and Caetano go to Salvador where they live with Rogério Duarte and the musician and philosopher Walter Smetak; Gil marries Sandra Gadelha; he records voice and guitar tracks for his next album in Salvador; in July, following a farewell concert, Gil and Caetano leave for exile in London with their spouses; "Aquele abraço," Gil's first commercial hit, is edited for release as a single.

1970 Gil and Caetano play a show together at Royal Festival Hall, in England, and perform in other European countries as well, including: France, Switzerland, Germany, Austria, Denmark, and Sweden; Pedro Gadelha Gil Moreira, Gil and Sandra's first son, is born; Gil is awarded the Golfinho de Ouro prize by the Museum of Image and Sound (MIS) in Rio de Janeiro in recognition of his song "Aquele abraço," but he refuses the award in an article published in *Pasquim*; Gil records the soundtrack for the film *Copacabana mon amour*, by Rogério Sganzerla.

1971 In London, Gil records an LP of songs in English, some in collaboration with the singer and writer Jorge Mautner.

1972   Gil returns to Brazil and releases the LP *Expresso 2222* as well as *Barra 69, Caetano e Gil ao vivo na Bahia no Teatro Castro Alves*, a live recording of Gil and Caetano's farewell concert prior to going into exile.

1973   Gil releases two songs that become major hits, "Meio-de-campo" and "Eu só quero um xodó"; the Brazilian dictatorship censors the song "Cálice," written by Gil and Chico Buarque.

1974   The live recording *Temporada de verão*, with Gil, Caetano, and Gal, is released; Preta Maria Gadelha Gil Moreira, Gil and Sandra's daughter, is born; Gil releases *Gilberto Gil ao vivo*.

1975   Gil releases the double album *Ogum Xangô* with Jorge Benjor; the landmark album *Refazenda* is also released.

1976   Maria Gadelha Gil Moreira, daughter of Gil and Sandra, is born; the LP *Doces Bárbaros* is released, recorded with Gil, Caetano Veloso, Gal Costa, and Maria Bethânia; on July 7th, while on tour in Florianópolis, Santa Catarina, Gil is detained for marijuana possession.

1978   Gil performs at the Montreux International Jazz Festival.

1979   In Salvador, Gil meets Flora Nair Giordano, who soon becomes his wife; Gil joins Maria Bethânia on the Conselho Estadual Cultural da Bahia (State Culture Committee); he releases the album *Realce*, the final album in the "Re-" trilogy.

1980   Gil performs a show with the Jamaican
reggae singer Jimmy Cliff.

1981   Releases the LPs *Luar* and *Brasil*, the latter of
which features João Gilberto with Gilberto
Gil, Caetano Veloso and Maria Bethânia.

1982   Releases the album *Um banda Um*.

1983   Releases the LP *Extra*.

1984   Releases the LP *Raça humana*.

1985   Performs in the Rock in Rio Festival; Bem Giordano
Gil Moreira, Gil and Flora's first son, is born; release
of the LP *Dia dorim noite neon*; Gil celebrates his 20
year anniversary as a professional musician with a
large event in São Paulo, organized by the poet and
lyricist Waly Salomão – *Gil, 20 anos luz*, consists of a
week of shows, debates, films, lectures, and activities.

1987   Gil moves to Salvador to take over the presidency of the
Fundação Gregório de Matos, which serves as a sort of
Municipal Culture Secretariat for the city.

1988   Isabela Giordano Gil Moreira, Gil and Flora's daughter,
is born; Gil leaves his position as president of the
Fundação Gregório de Matos to run for Mayor of
Salvador; after failing to receive the support of the
PMDB, Gil decides to run for a seat on City Council.

1989   Gil begins his term as a City Council member for the city of Salvador; he is elected chair of the Committee for Environmental Preservation and he presides over the *Negro-Mestiço* Reference Center; he creates the environmental movement Onda Azul to preserve the oceans; he releases his album *O Eterno Deus Mu Dança*.

1990   In January, Gil's son and drummer Pedro dies after a car accident at 19 years old.

1991   José Giordano Gil Moreira, Gil and Flora's third son, is born.

1992   The album *Parabolicamará* is released.

1993   Gil and Caetano release the album *Tropicália 2*.

1994   Gil performs a show for the program MTV Acoustic; the album is released internationally by Warner with the title *Gilberto Gil Unplugged*.

1996   The book *Gilberto Gil -Todas as letras* (Companhia das Letras), edited by Carlos Rennó, is published; the book includes Gil's reflections on the genesis of 80 of his songs.

1997   Gil releases the double album *Quanta*.

1998   The live double album *Quanta gente veio ver*, is released and wins the Grammy for World Music Album of the Year in 1999; the administration of recently-elected

President Fernando Henrique Cardoso explores naming
Gil as Minister of the Environment.

2000   Gil releases the album *Gilberto Gil e as canções de
"Eu tu eles,"* consisting mainly of Luiz Gonzaga songs
recorded for the soundtrack of Andrucha Waddington's
film; Gil also releases the CD *Gil Milton* (Warner),
recorded with MPB artist Milton Nascimento.

2001   Gil participates in Salvador's "Carnaval pela Paz"
with his own soundcar, Expresso 2222; he records
the album *Kaya N'Gan Daya* in Jamaica with
remakes of songs consecrated by Bob Marley.

2002   Os Doces Bárbaros reunite for a series of shows;
President Luiz Inácio Lula da Silva is elected and
nominates Gil as Brazilian Minister of Culture.

2003   Gil begins his term as Minister of Culture;
he performs the show *El sueño existe* in
Chile in homage to Salvador Allende.

2004   Gil participates on the panel "Creative Commons"
during the International Free Software Forum in Porto
Alegre.

2006   Wins the Grammy for Best Album of Música
Popular Brasileira for *Eletracústico*.

2008   Resigns from the position of Minister of Culture because
of difficulty maintaining an active artistic career.

| **2009** | Records and releases the live album *BandaDois*. |

| **2010** | Records the albums *Fé na festa* and *Fé na festa ao vivo*. |

| **2011** | Records the performance *Gil + 10* with a variety of invited artists |

| **2012** | Performs *Concerto de cordas & máquinas de ritmo*, as part of a a mini-tour throughout Brazil. |

| **2014** | Releases the album *Gilbertos Samba* and its live version, recorded at the Teatro Municipal de Niterói. |

| **2015** | Performs the show *Dois amigos, um século de música* alongside Caetano Veloso as part of an extensive national and international tour. |

| **2016** | Participates in the Opening Ceremony of the Olympic Games in Rio de Janeiro along with funk carioca singer Anitta and Caetano Veloso. |

| **2018** | Performs the show *Trinca de ases*, with Gal Costa and Nando Reis; Gil releases the album *Ok Ok Ok*, which wins the Latin Grammy for Best Album of Música Popular Brasileira the following year. |

| **2019** | Composes the songs for singer Roberta Sá's album *Giro*; Gil performs a show in Salvador alongside the band BaianaSystem which is later released as a digital album. |

| **2020** | In the midst of the COVID-19 pandemic, Gil performs a live birthday concert from quarantine |

in Araras (Rio de Janeiro state); the show is
streamed over YouTube and later released as a
digital album with the title *São João em Araras*.

2021 Gil is named a member of the
Academia Brasileira de Letras.

2022 Launches, through Amazon Prime, the
television program *At Home with the Gil's*,
a reality show about his family life.

BIOGRAPHICAL REFERENCES

A Cor do Som
Bahian instrumental music ensemble, formed in 1977 by Dadi Carvalho, Mu Carvalho, Gustavo Schroeter, Armandinho and Ary Dias.

Airto Moreira
(1941-). Percussionist from Santa Catarina state, married to jazz singer Flora Purim. Came to prominence in the 1960s as a member of Quarteto Novo with Hermeto Pascoal before moving to the United States.

Alan White
(1949-2022). English drummer, member of the 1970s progressive rock group Yes.

Alfredo Sirkis
(1950-2020). Journalist, writer, and politician from Rio de Janeiro. Served as president of the Brazilian Green Party and executive coordinator of the Brazilian Forum on Climate Change. Spent years in exile in Chile during the Brazilian military dictatorship.

Álvaro Guimarães
(1948-). Film director and designer from Bahia, edited the short-lived alternative periodical *Flor do Mal* in the early 1970s.

Alex Korner
(1928-1984). British guitarist, known as the "founder of British blues."

Ana Maria Bahiana
(1950-). Journalist from Rio de Janeiro based in Los Angeles. Considered an important figure in Brazilian music and film criticism.

Andrucha Waddington
(1970-). Director, producer, and screenwriter from Rio de Janeiro who directed *Eu, tu, eles*, a 2000 film that participated in the Cannes Film Festival.

Ângela Maria
(1929-2018). Abelim Maria da Cunha. Singer and actress from Rio de Janeiro. Iconic figure of the samba-canção genre. Elected "Queen of Radio" in 1954 by the Brazilian Radio Association.

Antônio Bivar
(1939-2020). São Paulo writer and playwright. Actively participated in the countercultural movements that began in the 1960s. In 1982, he organized O Começo do Fim do Mundo, one of Brazil's most important punk music festivals.

Antônio Callado
(1917-1997). Journalist, novelist, and playwright from Niterói. *Kuarup* is among one of his most important novels.

Arnaldo Brandão
(1951-). Singer, songwriter, and bassist from Rio de Janeiro. Member of A Bolha, the 1960s band that played with Gal Costa and others.

Ary Barroso
(1903-1964). Songwriter and radio pre-

senter from Minas Gerais who hosted Calouros em Desfile program for new talent. Among his compositions, "Aquarela do Brasil" stands out for having inaugurated the genre of "samba exaltação." Nominated for an Oscar for his song "Rio de Janeiro," composed for the 1944 film *Brazil*.

Augusto Calheiros
(1891-1956). Singer and songwriter from Northeastern Brazil who performed with Turunas de Mauricéia, a group that incorporated Northeastern rhythms into its music.

Augusto de Campos
(1931-). Poet, essayist, and translator from São Paulo. Creator of Brazilian concrete poetry movement, along with Haroldo de Campos and Décio Pignatari. In 2015, he was awarded the Pablo Neruda Ibero-American Poetry Prize.

Batatinha
(1924-1997). Stage name of Oscar da Penha. Bahian songwriter active in the genre of Bahian samba. Many of his compositions were made famous by singer Maria Bethânia.

Bob Nelson
(1918-2009). Nelson Roberto Perez. Singer and actor from São Paulo based in Rio de Janeiro, best known for singing country music.

Bruce Henri
(1949-). Bruce Henry Leitman. US-born bass player who moved to Brazil during the 1960s, accompanying numerous jazz and MPB artists including Gilberto Gil and Caetano Veloso.

Caetano Veloso
(1942). Singer and songwriter from Bahia, one of the most influential popular musicians of the 20th and 21st centuries. One of the prime movers of the Tropicalist movement of the late 1960s, and author of *Verdade Tropical* (1997), an important reflection on Brazilian popular music.

Carlos Cachaça
(1902-1999). Nickname of Carlos Moreira de Castro. Samba songwriter and one of the founders of Mangueira Samba School in Rio de Janeiro.

Carlos Castañeda
(1925-1998). Peruvian-born author of the popular but discredited books *Teachings of Don Juan* and *Journey to Ixtlan*, written while studying anthropology at UCLA in the 1960s and 70s.

Carlos Galhardo
(1913-1985). Brazilian singer, son of Italians, born in Buenos Aires. Considered a central figure of the radio era.

Carlos Rennó
(1956-). Lyricist and music producer from São Paulo, active during the "vanguarda

paulista" in the 1980s. Collaborated with many Brazilian songwriters, including Gilberto Gil, Arrigo Barnabé, and others.

Cartola
(1908-1980). Nickname of Agenor de Oliveira. Singer and songwriter from Rio de Janeiro. Considered one of the greatest samba composers; founding member of Mangueira Samba School.

César Lattes
(1924-2005). Cesare Mansueto Giulio Lattes. Physicist from Paraná, co-founder of the Centro Brasileiro de Pesquisas Físicas whose research focused primarily on cosmic radiation. One of the discoverers of the pion subatomic particle.

Chico Buarque
(1944-). Singer and songwriter in the MPB genre whose songs are well-known for their lyricism and political critique. An award-winning novelist, winner of the Prêmio Camões in 2019.

Chris Bennett
(1948-). US jazz and pop singer based in Los Angeles.

Claudio Prado
(1951). Intellectual, cultural theorist, and music producer from São Paulo. Influential theorist of digital culture who also produced shows by Os Mutantes and others during the 1970s.

Dalva de Oliveira
(1917-1072). Singer and composer from São Paulo. Central figure during the golden age of Brazilian radio. Named "Queen of Radio" in 1951. Recorded more than 400 songs and performed on several Carmen Miranda albums.

David Gilmour
(1946-). English guitarist, singer, songwriter who joined the band Pink Floyd in 1967.

Décio Pignatari
(1927-2012). Poet and advertiser from São Paulo, considered one of the central figures in the Brazilian concrete poetry movement of the 1950s.

Dominguinhos
(1941-2013). Artistic name of José Domingo de Morais Accordionist, singer, and songwriter from Pernambuco. Considered the artistic heir to Luiz Gonzaga, with whom he studied form a young age. Latin Grammy winner in 2002 and 2012.

Donga
(1890-1974). Artistic name of Ernesto Joaquim Maria dos Santos. Songwriter and guitarist from Rio de Janeiro who performed in the choro/samba group Os Oito Batutas. Credited with composing the first recorded samba, "Pelo Telefone," in 1916.

Dorival Caymmi
(1914-2008). Singer and songwriter from Bahia whose songs focused on the culture and day-to-day life of his state. A major point of reference for the bossa nova movement, his major hits include "Saudade da Bahia," Samba da Minha Terra," "Doralice," and "Maracangalha."

Edu Lobo
(1943-). Songwriter, arranger and guitarist from Rio de Janeiro associated with the bossa nova movement, his songs include collaborations with Vinicius de Moraes and Chico Buarque.

Elis Regina
(1945-1982). Singer from Rio Grande do Sul, best known for her performances and recordings of bossa nova and MPB.

Elizeth Cardoso
(1920-1990). Singer of samba, samba-canção, and bossa nova. In 1958, she recorded *Canção de Amor Demais*, an album that included compositions by Tom Jobim and Vinicius de Moraes, as well as guitar playing of João Gilberto, widely considered the first bossa nova album.

Emilinha Borba
(1923-2005). Emília Savana de Sousa Costa da Silva Borba. Singer of samba, choro and marches, from Rio de Janeiro. Carmen Miranda's artistic goddaughter, named "Queen of Radio" by Brazilian Radio Association in 1953.

Erasmo Carlos
(1941-2022). Singer and songwriter from Rio de Janeiro. A central figure in the 1960s Brazilian rock movement Jovem Guarda. Many of his most popular songs were written in collaboration with his frequent songwriting partner Roberto Carlos.

Ferreira Gullar
(1930-2016). José Ribamar Ferreira. Poet, chronicler, playwright and art critic from Maranhão, one of the founders of the neo-concrete poetry movement. Member of the Brazilian Academy of Letters, awarded the Camões Prize in 2010.

Francisco Alves
(1898-1952). Singer born in Rio de Janeiro. Considered one of the most important singers of the Golden Age of Brazilian radio; sang on the first recording of "Aquarela do Brasil."

Gal Costa
(1945-2022). Artistic name of Maria das Graças. Singer from Bahia who participated in Tropicália and Doces Bárbaros, in addition to having a prolific solo career beginning in the 1960s.

Geraldo Vandré
(1935-). Singer and songwriter of protest music from Paraíba state, rose to prominence during the televised Brazilian music festivals of the 1960s with political songs such as "Disparada" and "Pra Não Dizer Que Não Falei Das Flores."

Glauber Rocha

(1939-1981). Bahian filmmaker and central figure of Cinema Novo, a movement that emerged during the 1950s and 60s focusing on realism and social commentary.

Guilherme Araújo

(1936-2007). Producer from Rio de Janeiro who worked with figures such as Gal Costa, Gilberto Gil, and Caetano Veloso.

Hans-Joachim Koellreutter

(1915-2005). German art music composer and musicologist. Helped found the Escola Livre de Música de São Paulo (1952) and the School of Music of the Universidade Federal da Bahia (1954). One of the founders of the Brazilian Música Viva movement.

Hélio Oiticica

(1937-1980). Visual artist from Rio de Janeiro known for immersive artworks that involved the spectator as participant. Key source of inspiration for the Tropicalist movement whose 1967 installation Tropicália gave the movement its name.

Hermeto Pascoal

(1936-). Composer and virtuosic multi-instrumentalist from Alagoas state, widely recognized as a pioneering figure in Brazilian "música instrumental."

Irmãs Batista

Dircinha Batista

(1922-1999). Actress and singer from São Paulo. Performer of carnival songs who, together with her sister Linda, broke sales records in the 1940s and 1950s.

Linda Batista

(1919-1988). São Paulo singer and composer. In 1937, she was the first singer to be elected "Queen of Radio" by the Brazilian Radio Association, a title she held for eleven consecutive years.

Jackson do Pandeiro

(1919-1982). Stage name of José Gomes Filho. Singer and songwriter from Paraíba who combined rhythmic Northeastern genres, such as baião, xote, forró and coco, with samba.

Jair Rodrigues

(1939-2014). Singer from São Paulo, co-host of the television program O Fino da Bossa (1965-1967) with singer Elis Regina.

Jararaca

(1986-1977). Stage name of José Luís Rodrigues Calazans. Singer, songwriter, and comedian based in Pernambuco. Became famous for his work as part of the duo Jararaca e Ratinho. Composed the well-known carnival march "Mamãe eu quero" (1934).

Jim Capaldi

(1944-2005). English drummer and co-founder of the progressive rock group Traffic in 1967.

Jimmy Cliff
(1944-). Jamaican singer and songwriter, one of the most iconic figures in reggae. Starred in the 1972 film *The Harder They Come*.

João Gilberto
(1931-2019) Singer and guitarist from Bahia, one of the founding members of the bossa nova movement.

John Mayall
(1933-). English singer and guitarist, founder of the 1960s band John Mayall and the Bluesbreakers. One of the central figures in blues music in the UK.

Jom Tob Azulay
(1941). Filmmaker from Rio de Janeiro who directed Os Doces Bárbaros (1976), a documentary about the group's tour of Brazil.

Jorge Ben Jor
(1945-). Singer, songwriter, and guitarist from Rio de Janeiro. His album Samba Esquema Novo inaugurated a new style that later shaped the genres known as sambalanço and samba-rock. Considered one of the top 5 greatest Brazilian musicians by *Rolling Stone* magazine in 2008.

Jorge Goulart
(1926-2012). Jorge Neves Bastos. Singer from Rio de Janeiro, active in the 1940s and 1950s revue theater and cinema. A communist militant, he was forced into exile with his wife Nora Ney (also a singer) following the military coup of 1964.

Jorge Mautner
(1941-). Henrique George Mautner. Singer, songwriter, and author from Rio de Janeiro, best known for his song "Maracatu Atômico." Winner of a 2003 Latin Grammy Award for album co-written with Caetano Veloso.

José Agrippino de Paula
(1937-2007). Writer from São Paulo whose book *PanAmérica* (1967) stands out as particularly Tropicalist due to its irreverence and the dialogue it establishes with mass culture figures.

José Carlos Capinan
(1941-). Bahian poet and lyricist. Actively participated in the Tropicalist movement, writing lyrics for several of its members.

Juca Ferreira
(1941-). João Luiz Silva Ferreira. Bahian sociologist and politician who served as Minister of Culture during President Lula and Dilma Rousseff's administrations.

Júlio Medaglia
(1938-). Maestro and composer from São Paulo, one of the creators of the Música Nova Manifesto in 1961. Student of Pierre Boulez and Karlheinz Stockhausen.

Lia de Itamaracá
(1944-). Stage name of Maria Madalena Correia do Nascimento. Singer and songwriter from Pernambuco. Best-known representative of the ciranda, a folkloric ring dance from the Northeast.

Lina Bo Bardi
(1914-1992). Italian-Brazilian architect. Central figure in Brazilian modernist architecture who designed the Museum of Contemporary Art of São Paulo (MASP) and helped renovate the historic center of Salvador in the 1980s.

Luiz Gonzaga
(1912-1989). Songwriter, singer, accordionist from Pernambuco. Known as the "King of the Baião," recorded popular "forró" music from Northeastern Brazil and broke record sales during the 1940s and 1950s.

Maria Bethânia
(1946). Bahian singer, member of the "grupo baiano" cohort that included her brother, Caetano Veloso. Central figure in the Tropicália movement.

Mário de Andrade
(1893-1945). Poet, novelist, and musicologist from São Paulo. Active in the Brazilian modernist movement of the 1920s, recorded Brazilian folk music, and wrote the famous novel *Macunaíma*·(1928).

Mário Schenberg
(1914-1990). Physicist and art critic from Pernambuco state who made contributions to quantum physics and astrophysics.

Marlene
(1922-2014). Stage name of Victória Bonaiuti Delfino dos Santos. Singer and actress born in São Paulo. Selected as "Queen of Radio" by the Brazilian Radio Association in 1949.

Mauro de Almeida
(1882-1956). Playwright, journalist, and songwriter from Rio de Janeiro.

MPB4
Vocal group founded in 1964 in Rio de Janeiro by Miltinho, Magro, Aquiles, and Ruy Faria.

Nana Caymmi
(1941-). Singer from Rio de Janeiro, daughter of Bahian singer-songwriter Dorival Caymmi.

Nara Leão
(1942-1989). Brazilian singer from Espírito Santo state who began her career in bossa nova before expanding to other genres and musical movements, including Tropicália and political song, including the show Opinião.

Nelson Jacobina
(1953-2012). Guitarist and songwriter from Rio de Janeiro, one of the main creative partners of multi-instrumentalist Jorge Mautner.

Nelson Motta

(1944-). Journalist, writer, and songwriter from São Paulo who also produced shows of MPB icons Elis Regina and Gal Costa.

Nik Turner

(1940-2022). English flautist and saxophonist, founding member of the 1970s space rock band Hawkwind.

Orlando Silva

(1915-1978). Singer of sambas and samba-canções from Rio de Janeiro, considered one of the most important Brazilian radio performers of the 1930s and 40s.

Os Mutantes

Psychedelic rock band founded in 1967 with lead singer Rita Lee and brothers Arnaldo Baptista and Sergio Dias.

Oswald de Andrade

(1890-1954). Poet, essayist, and playwright from São Paulo. Central figure in the Brazilian modernist movement, one of the main figures in the 1922 "Modern Art Week" in São Paulo. Author of the famous "Brazil-Wood Manifesto" (1924) and "Cannibalist Manifesto" (1928).

Paulinho da Viola

(1942). Songwriter, guitarist, and singer from Rio de Janeiro. Considered a central figure in the genre of samba, with compositions that include the well-known "Coração Leviano."

Paulo Francis

(1930-1997). Franz Paul Trannin da Matta Heilborn. Journalist and writer from Rio de Janeiro whose acerbic critiques of Brazilian culture have made him a controversial figure.

Pepeu Gomes

(1952-). Electric guitarist, singer, and songwriter from Bahia who founded the MPB-rock group Novos Baianos in 1969.

Perfeito Fortuna

(1950-). Perfeito Antônio Fortuna Serra Lopes. Luso-Brazilian actor and cultural producer. Member of the counter-cultural theater company Asdrubal Trouxe o Trombone. Founder of the iconic Circo Voador and Fundição Progresso performance venues in Rio de Janeiro.

Regina Echeverria

(1951-). Journalist from São Paulo best-known for her biographies of Brazilian musicians including Elis Regina, Cazuza, and others.

Roberto Carlos

(1941-). Singer and songwriter from the state of Espírito Santo, a leading figure in the 1964 Brazilian rock movement Jovem Guarda. Well-known internationally as a singer of romantic song.

Roberto Menescal

(1937). Musician and songwriter, born in Espírito Santo state. Considered a founding member of the bossa nova movement. His best-known songs include "O barquinho" and "Nós e o mar," composed with Ronaldo Bôscoli.

Rogério Duarte
(1939-2016). Bahian graphic designer, illustrator, and musician. Considered a key intellectual figure within the Tropicalist movement. His works include the iconic poster for the film *Deus e o Diabo na terra do sol* (1964).

Rogério Duprat
(1932-2006). Maestro, arranger, and composer from Rio de Janeiro, one of the creators of the Música Nova manifesto in 1961 and a key collaborator in the Tropicália movement.

Rogério Sganzerla
(1946-2004). Filmmaker from Santa Catarina state. Central figure in the 1960s and 1970s experimental genre known as Cinema Marginal, which includes his film, *O bandido da luz vermelha* (1968).

Ronnie Von
(1944-). Singer, songwriter, and television presenter from Rio de Janeiro, considered one of the central figures in the Brazilian rock movement Jovem Guarda.

Rubens Gerchman
(1942-2008). Visual artist from Rio de Janeiro associated with several avant garde movements, including pop art and concrete and neo-concrete art.

Ruy Guerra
(1931–). Ruy Alexandre Guerra Coelho Pereira. Mozambican director and screenwriter based in Brazil. Central figure of the Cinema Novo movement whose most acclaimed films include *Os cafajestes* (1962) and *Os fuzis* (1964). Composed lyrics with Chico Buarque, Milton Nascimento, Edu Lobo, among others.

Sérgio Mendes
(1941-). Brazilian pianist who helped popularize bossa nova and MPB in the US. Best known for his recordings with the group Brasil '66, including the Jorge Ben song "Mas que nada."

Sérgio Ricardo
(1932-2020). Pianist and songwriter from São Paulo associated with Brazil's Cinema Novo movement. Composed the soundtrack for the films *Deus e o Diabo na terra do sol* (1964) and *Terra em transe* (1967), and worked as an actor and film director.

Sidney Miller
(1945-1980). Sidney Álvaro Miller Filho. Songwriter from Rio de Janeiro who gained prominence during the televised song festivals of the 1960s.

Syd Barrett
(1946-2006). English singer, songwriter, and guitarist. One of the founding members of Pink Floyd.

Tom Zé

(1937-). Antonio José Santana Martins. Singer, songwriter, and multi-instrumentalist from Bahia who participated in the Tropicália movement. Best known for satirical song lyrics and for musical experimentalism, including the invention of new instruments.

Torquato Neto

(1948-1972). Poet and lyricist from Piauí. Key figure in the conceptualization of the Tropicalist movement.

Tutty Moreno

(1947-). Drummer from Bahia who accompanied major names in Brazilian popular music including Gilberto Gil and Jards Macalé. Married to the singer and songwriter Joyce Moreno.

Vanusa

(1947-2020). Vanusa Santos Flores. Singer and songwriter from São Paulo who participated in the 1960s Jovem Guarda movement before going on to have a prolific career as a solo recording artist.

Vicente Celestino

(1894-1968). Singer and early recording artist from Rio de Janeiro whose songs include "O Ébrio," which inspired the 1946 film of the same name, directed by his wife Gilda de Abreu.

Walter Smetak

(1913-1984). Swiss avant-garde composer, cellist, and writer who taught at the Universidade Federal da Bahia during the 1960s, influencing a generation of young Brazilian popular musicians.

Wanderléa

(1944-). Wanderléa Charlup Boere Salim. Singer from Minas Gerais state who rose to prominence as part of the Jovem Guarda movement and became known for her recordings of hit songs such as "Ternura."

Zé Celso Martinez Corrêa

(1937-). São Paulo theater director, playwright, and actor. Directed the iconic experimental theater group Teatro Oficina.

Zé Vicente

(1947-2005). José Vicente de Paula. Playwright from Minas Gerais state, considered an important figure in the evolution of the Nova Dramaturgia movement of the 1960s and 70s. His best-known works include the 1971 play *Hoje é Dia de Rock.*

DISCOGRAPHY

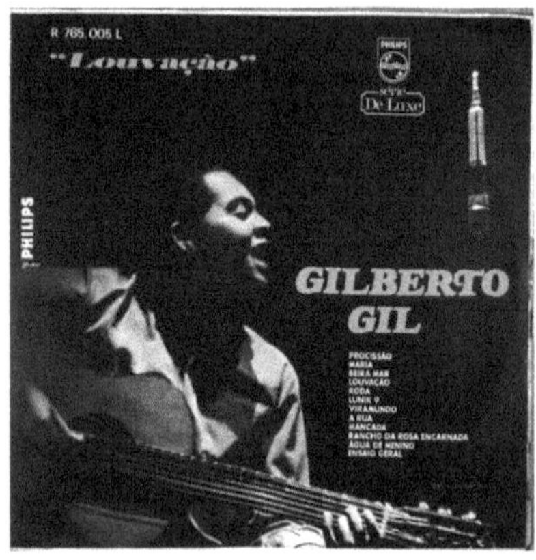

1967
LOUVAÇÃO

Label: Philips — R 765.005 L

SIDE A

1. Louvação (Gilberto Gil, Torquato Neto)
2. Beira Mar (Gilberto Gil, Caetano Veloso)
3. Lunik 9 (Gilberto Gil)
4. Ensaio Geral (Gilberto Gil)
5. Maria (Gilberto Gil)
6. A Rua (Gilberto Gil, Torquato Neto)

SIDE B

1. Roda (Gilberto Gil, João Augusto)
2. Rancho da Rosa Encarnada (Gilberto Gil, Torquato Neto, Geraldo Vandré)
3. Viramundo (Gilberto Gil, Capinan)
4. Mancada (Gilberto Gil)
5. Água de Meninos (Gilberto Gil, Capinan)
6. Procissão (Gilberto Gil)

**1968
GILBERTO GIL**

Label: Philips — R 765.024 L
Producer: Manuel Barebein
Arrangements: Rogério Duprat
Special guests:
Os Mutantes

SIDE A
1. Frevo Rasgado (Gilberto Gil, Bruno Ferreira)
2. Coragem Pra Suportar (Gilberto Gil)
3. Domingou (Gilberto Gil, Torquato Neto)
4. Marginália II (Gilberto Gil, Torquato Neto)
5. Pega a Voga, Cabeludo (Gilberto Gil, Juan Arcon)

SIDE B
1. Ele Falava Nisso Todo Dia (Gilberto Gil)
2. Procissão (Gilberto Gil)
3. Luzia Luluza (Gilberto Gil)
4. Pé da Roseira (Gilberto Gil)
5. Domingo No Parque (Gilberto Gil)

1968
TROPICÁLIA
OU PANIS ET CIRCENSIS

Label: Philips — R 765.040 L
Arrangements: Rogério Duprat

SIDE A

1. Miserere Nobis (Gilberto Gil, Capinan) Singer: Gilberto Gil
2. Coração Materno (Vicente Celestino) Singer: Caetano Veloso
3. Panis Et Circenses (Caetano Veloso, Gilberto Gil). Singers: Os Mutantes
4. Lindonéia (Caetano Veloso) Singer: Nara Leão
5. Parque Industrial (Tom Zé) Singers: Tom Zé, Caetano Veloso, Gal Costa, Gilberto Gil, Os Mutantes
6. Geleia Geral (Gilberto Gil, Torquato Neto) Singer: Gilberto Gil

SIDE B

1. Baby (Caetano Veloso) Singer: Gal Costa, Caetano Veloso
2. Três Caravelas (Las Tres Carabelas) (A. Algueró Jr., E. Moreu, Adapt. João de Barro) Singers: Caetano Veloso, Gilberto Gil
3. Enquanto Seu Lobo Não Vem (Caetano Veloso) Singer: Caetano Veloso
4. Mamãe, Coragem (Caetano Veloso, Torquato Neto) Singer: Gal Costa
5. Bat Macumba (Gilberto Gil, Caetano Veloso) Singer: Gilberto Gil
6. Hino ao Senhor do Bonfim (João A. Wanderley, Petion de Vilar) Singers: Caetano Veloso, Gilberto Gil, Gal Costa, Os Mutantes

1969
GILBERTO GIL

Label: Philips — R 765.087 L
Producer: Manuel Barebein
Arrangements: Rogério Duprat

SIDE A

1. Cérebro Eletrônico (Gilberto Gil)
2. Volks Volkswagem Blue (Gilberto Gil)
3. Aquele Abraço (Gilberto Gil)
4. Dezessete Léguas E Meia (Humberto Teixeira, Carlos Barroso)
5. A Voz do Vivo (Caetano Veloso)

SIDE B

1. Vitrines (Gilberto Gil)
2. 2001 (Rita Lee, Tom Zé)
3. Futurível (Gilberto Gil)
4. Objeto Semi-identificado (Rogério Duarte, Gilberto Gil, Rogério Duprat)

1971
GILBERTO GIL

Label: Philips — 6349 006
Producer: Ralph Mace

SIDE A

1. Nega (Photograph Blues) (Gilberto Gil)
2. Can't Find My Way Home (Steve Winwood)
3. The Three Mushrooms (Gilberto Gil, Jorge Mautner)
4. Babylon (Gilberto Gil, Jorge Mautner)

SIDE B

1. Volks Volkswagem Blue (Gilberto Gil)
2. Mamma (Gilberto Gil)
3. One O'Clock Last Morning 20th April 1970 (Gilberto Gil)
4. Crazy Pop Rock (Gilberto Gil, Jorge Mautner)

**1972
BARRA 69**

Label: Pirata Philips — 1401
Producers: Paulo Lima and
Roberto Santana
Records of Caetano Veloso
Veloso and Gilberto Gil in Bahia
on July 20th and 21st, 1969

SIDE A
1. Cinema Olympia (Caetano Veloso) Singer: Caetano Veloso
2. Frevo Rasgado (Gilberto Gil, Bruno Ferreira) Singer: Gilberto Gil
3. Superbacana (Caetano Veloso) Singer: Caetano Veloso
4. Madalena (Entra Em Beco, Sai Em Beco) (Isidoro, Adpt. Gilberto Gil)
Singer: Gilberto Gil

SIDE B
1. Atrás do Trio Elétrico (Caetano Veloso) Singer: Caetano Veloso
2. Domingo No Parque (Gilberto Gil) Singer: Gilberto Gil
3. Alegria, Alegria (Caetano Veloso); Hino do Esporte Clube Bahia (Adroaldo
Ribeiro Costa); Aquele Abraço (Gilberto Gil)
Singers: Caetano Veloso e Gilberto Gil

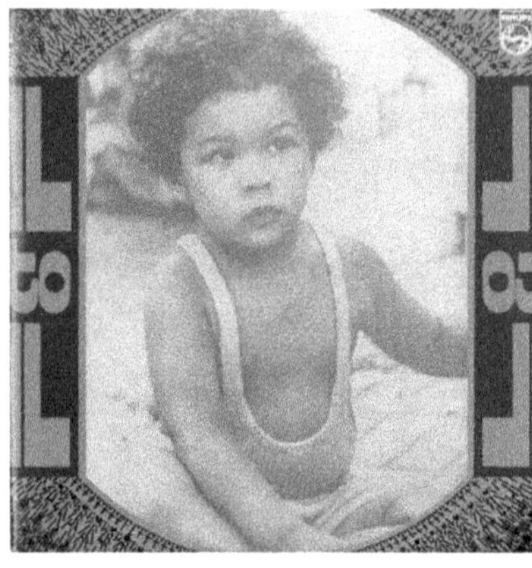

1969
EXPRESSO 2222

Label: Philips — 6349 034
Producer: Guilherme Araújo

SIDE A

1. Pipoca Moderna (Caetano Veloso, Sebastião Biano)
Featuring: Banda de Pífanos de Caruaru
2. Back In Bahia (Gilberto Gil)
3. O Canto da Ema (Alventino Cavalcanti, Aires Viana, João do Vale)
4. Chiclete Com Banana (Gordurinha, Almira Castilho)
5. Ele e Eu (Gilberto Gil)

SIDE B

1. Sai do Sereno (Onildo Almeida) Featuring: Gal Costa
2. Expresso 2222 (Gilberto Gil)
3. O Sonho Acabou (Gilberto Gil)
4. Oriente (Gilberto Gil)

1974
GILBERTO GIL AO VIVO

Label: Philips — 6349 124
Producer: Guilherme Araújo
Arrangements: Perinho Albu-
querque
Recorded live at TUCA -
São Paulo, October 1974

SIDE A

1. João Sabino (Gilberto Gil)
2. Abra o Olho (Gilberto Gil)
3. Lugar Comum (João Donato, Gilberto Gil)

SIDE B

1. Menina Goiaba (Gilberto Gil)
2. Sim, Foi Você (Caetano Veloso)
3. Herói das Estrelas (Nelson Jacobina, Jorge Mautner)

1974
TEMPORADA DE VERÃO

Label: Philips — 6349 108
Producer: Guilherme Araújo
Arrangements: Perinho Albuquerque
Artists: Gilberto Gil, Caetano Veloso and Gal Costa
Recorded live at the Vila Velha Theater - Salvador, from January 10 to February 22, 1974.

SIDE A

1. Quem Nasceu (Péricles Cavalcanti) Singer: Gal Costa
2. De Noite Na Cama (Caetano Veloso) Singer: Caetano Veloso
3. O Conteúdo (Caetano Veloso) Singer: Caetano Veloso
4. Terremoto (João Donato, Paulo César Pinheiro) Singer: Gilberto Gil

SIDE B

1. O Relógio Quebrou (Jorge Mautner) Singer: Gilberto Gil
2. O Sonho Acabou (Gilberto Gil) Singer: Gilberto Gil
3. Cantiga do Sapo (Jackson do Pandeiro, Buco do Pandeiro)
Singer: Gilberto Gil
4. Acontece (Cartola) Singer: Gal Costa
5. Felicidade (Lupicínio Rodrigues) Singer: Caetano Veloso

1975
GIL E JORGE
OGUM XANGÔ

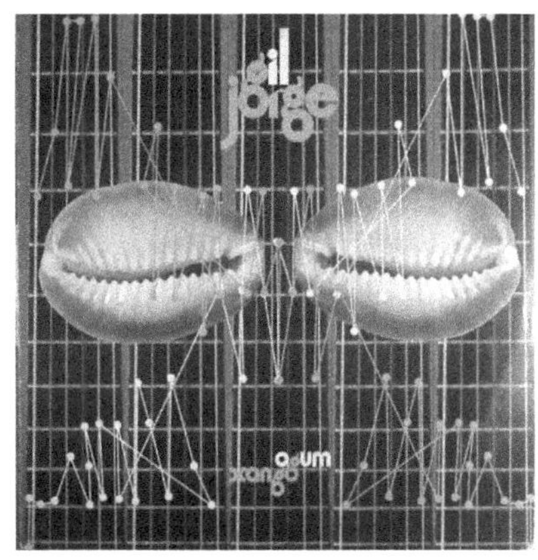

Label: Philips — 9299 453/4
Producers: Paulinho Tapajós and
Perinho Albuquerque
Artists: Gilberto Gil and
Jorge Ben Jor

SIDE A
1. Meu Glorioso São Cristóvão (Jorge Ben Jor)
2. Nega (Photograph Blues) (Gilberto Gil)

SIDE B
3. Jurubeba (Gilberto Gil)
4. Quem Mandou (Pé Na Estrada) (Jorge Ben Jor)

SIDE C
1. Taj Mahal (Jorge Ben Jor)
2. Morre o Burro Fica o Homem (Jorge Ben Jor)
3. Essa É Pra Tocar no Rádio (Gilberto Gil)

SIDE D
4. Filhos de Gandhi (Gilberto Gil)
5. Sarro (Gilberto Gil, Jorge Ben Jor)

1975
REFAZENDA

Label: Philips — 6349 152
Producer: Mazzola
Arrangements: Perinho
Albuquerque

SIDE A

1. Ela (Gilberto Gil)
2. Tenho Sede (Dominguinhos, Anastácia)
3. Refazenda (Gilberto Gil)
4. Pai e Mãe (Gilberto Gil)
5. Jeca Total (Gilberto Gil)
6. Essa É Pra Tocar no Rádio (Gilberto Gil)

SIDE B

1. Ê Povo Ê (Gilberto Gil)
2. Retiros Espirituais (Gilberto Gil)
3. O Rouxinol (Gilberto Gil, Jorge Mautner)
4. Lamento Sertanejo (Dominguinhos, Gilberto Gil)
5. Meditação (Gilberto Gil)

1975
DOCES BÁRBAROS
(DISCO 1)

Label: Philips — 6349 307/8
Producer: Perinho Albuquerque
Artists: Caetano Veloso, Gal
Costa, Gilberto Gil and
Maria Bethânia

SIDE A
1. Os Mais Doces Bárbaros (Caetano Veloso)
2. Fé Cega, Faca Amolada (Milton Nascimento, Ronaldo Bastos)
3. Atiraste Uma Pedra (Herivelto Martins, David Nasser)
4. Pássaro Proibido (Caetano Veloso, Maria Bethânia)

SIDE B
1. Chuck Berry Fields Forever (Gilberto Gil)
2. Gênesis (Caetano Veloso)
3. Tarasca Guidon (Waly Salomão)

1975
DOCES BÁRBAROS
(DISCO 2)

Label: Philips — 6349 307/8
Producer: Perinho Albuquerque
Artists: Caetano Veloso, Gal
Costa, Gilberto Gil and
Maria Bethânia

SIDE A

1. Eu e Ela Estávamos Ali Encostados na Parede (Gilberto Gil)
2. Esotérico (Gilberto Gil)
3. Eu Te Amo (Caetano Veloso)
4. O Seu Amor (Gilberto Gil)
5. Quando (Gal Costa, Caetano Veloso, Gilberto Gil)

SIDE B

1. Pé Quente Cabeça Fria (Gilberto Gil)
2. Peixe (Caetano Veloso)
3. Um Índio (Caetano Veloso)
4. São João Xangô Menino (Caetano Veloso, Gilberto Gil)
5. Nós Por Exemplo (Gilberto Gil)
6. Os Mais Doces Bárbaros (Caetano Veloso)

1977
REFAVELA

Label: Philips — 6349 329
Producer: Roberto Sant'Ana
Arrangements: Perinho Santana

SIDE A

1. Refavela (Gilberto Gil)
2. Ilê Ayê (Paulinho Camafeu)
3. Aqui e Agora (Gilberto Gil)
4. Norte da Saudade (Perinho Santana, Moacir Albuquerque, Gilberto Gil)
5. Babá Alapalá (Gilberto Gil)

SIDE B

1. Sandra (Gilberto Gil)
2. Samba do Avião (Tom Jobim)
3. Era Nova (Gilberto Gil)
4. Balafon (Gilberto Gil)
5. Patuscada de Gandhi (Afoxé Filhos de Gandhi)

1977
REFESTANÇA
GILBETO GIL E RITA LEE
AO VIVO

Label: Som Livre — 403.6137
Producer: Guto Graça Mello
Artists: Gilberto Gil and
Rita Lee

SIDE A

1. Refestança (Rita Lee, Gilberto Gil) Singers: Gilberto Gil, Rita Lee
2. É Proibido Fumar (Roberto Carlos, Erasmo Carlos)
Singers: Gilberto Gil, Rita Lee
3. Odara (Caetano Veloso) Singer: Gilberto Gil
4. Domingo No Parque (Gilberto Gil) Singer: Gilberto Gil
5. Back In Bahia (Gilberto Gil) Singer: Rita Lee
6. Giló (Rita Lee) Singer: Rita Lee

SIDE B

1. Ovelha Negra (Rita Lee) Singer: Gilberto Gil
2. Eu Só Quero Um Xodó (Dominguinhos, Anastácia) Singer: Gilberto Gil
3. De Leve (Get Back) (John Lennon, Paul McCartney, Adapt. Gilberto Gil,
Rita Lee) Singers: Rita Lee, Gilberto Gil
4. Arrombou A Festa (Rita Lee, Paulo Coelho) Singer: Rita Lee
5. Refestança (Rita Lee, Gilberto Gil) Singers: Gilberto Gil, Rita Lee

1978
AO VIVO EM MONTREUX

Label: WEA — BR 22.011/2
Producer: Mazzola

SIDE A

1. Chuck Berry Fields Forever (Gilberto Gil)

2. Chororô (Gilberto Gil)

SIDE A

1. São João Xangô Menino (Caetano Veloso, Gilberto Gil)

2. Respeita Januário (Luiz Gonzaga, Humberto Teixeira)

SIDE A

1. Ela (Gilberto Gil)

2. Bat Macumba (Gilberto Gil, Caetano Veloso); Exaltação À Mangueira (Enéas Brites da Silva, Aloísio Augusto da Costa)

SIDE A

1. Procissão (Gilberto Gil); Atrás do Trio Elétrico (Caetano Veloso); Mamãe Eu Quero (Jararaca, Vicente Paiva)

2. Triole (jam session) Featuring: Ivinho, Patrick Moraz, A Cor do Som

1978
**ANTOLOGIA DO
SAMBA-CHORO**

Label: Philips — 6349 361
Artists: Gilberto Gil and
Germano Mathias

SIDE A

1. Acertei No Milhar (Wilson Batista, Geraldo Pereira) Singer: Gilberto Gil
2. Falso Rebolado (Venâncio, Jorge Costa) Singer: Germano Mathias
3. Escurinho (Geraldo Pereira) Singer: Gilberto Gil
4. Minha Pretinha (Jair Gonçalves, Edson Borges) Singer: Germano Mathias
5. Senhor Delegado (Antoninho Lopes, Jaú) Singer: Germano Mathias

SIDE B

1. Minha Nega na Janela (Germano Mathias, Doca) Singer: Gilberto Gil
2. Não Volto Pra Casa (Denis Brean, Osvaldo Guilherme) Singer: Germano Mathias
3. A Situação Do Escurinho (Aldacir Louro, Padeirinho) Singer: Gilberto Gil
4. Rua (Jair Gonçalves) Singer: Germano Mathias
5. Samba Rubro-Negro (Wilson Batista, Jorge de Castro) Singer: Gilberto Gil

1979
REALCE

Label: Elektra WEA — BR 32.038
Producer: Mazzola

SIDE A
1. Realce (Gilberto Gil)
2. Sarará Miolo (Gilberto Gil)
3. Super-Homem (A Canção) (Gilberto Gil)
4. Tradição (Gilberto Gil)
5. Marina (Dorival Caymmi)

SIDE B
1. Rebento (Gilberto Gil)
2. Toda Menina Baiana (Gilberto Gil)
3. Logunedé (Gilberto Gil)
4. Nao Chore Mais (No Woman, No Cry) (Vincent Ford, Adapt. Gilberto Gil)

1979
NIGHTINGALE

Label: Warner — 6E-167
Producer: Sergio Mendes

SIDE A

1. Sarará Miolo (Gilberto Gil)
2. Goodbye My Girl (Péricles Santana, Gilberto Gil, Moacir Albuquerque)
3. Ela (Ella) (Gilberto Gil, Adapt. Carol Rogers)
4. Here And Now (Gilberto Gil)
5. Balafon (Gilberto Gil)

SIDE B

1. Alapalá The Myth Of Shango (Gilberto Gil, Adapt. Carol Rogers)
2. Maracatu Atômico (Jorge Mautner, Nelson Jacobina)
3. Move Along With Me (Gilberto Gil)
4. Nightingale (Gilberto Gil, Jorge Mautner)
5. Samba de Los Angeles (Gilberto Gil)

1981
BRASIL

Label: WEA — BR 38.045
Producers: André Midani and
Guto Graça Mello
Arrangements: Johnny Mandel
Artists: João Gilberto, Caetano
Veloso, Gilberto Gil and Maria
Bethânia

SIDE A
1. Aquarela do Brasil (Ary Barroso)
2. Disse Alguém (All Of Me) (Seymour Simons, Gerald Marks,
Adapt. Haroldo Barbosa)
3. Bahia Com H (Denis Brean)

SIDE B
1. No Tabuleiro da Baiana (Ary Barroso)
2. Milagre (Dorival Caymmi)
3. Cordeiro de Nanã (Mateus Aleluia, Dadinho)

1981
LUAR
(A GENTE PRECISA
VER O LUAR)

Label: WEA — BR 36.180
Producer: Liminha

SIDE A

1. A Gente Precisa Ver O Luar (Gilberto Gil)
2. Palco (Gilberto Gil)
3. Sonho Molhado (Gilberto Gil)
4. Lente do Amor (Gilberto Gil)
5. Morena (Gilberto Gil, Cassiano)

SIDE B

1. Cara A Cara (Caetano Veloso)
2. Cores Vivas (Gilberto Gil)
3. Axé Baba (Gilberto Gil)
4. Flora (Gilberto Gil)
5. Se Eu Quiser Falar Com Deus (Gilberto Gil)

1982
UM BANDA UM

Label: WEA — BR 26.063
Producer: Liminha

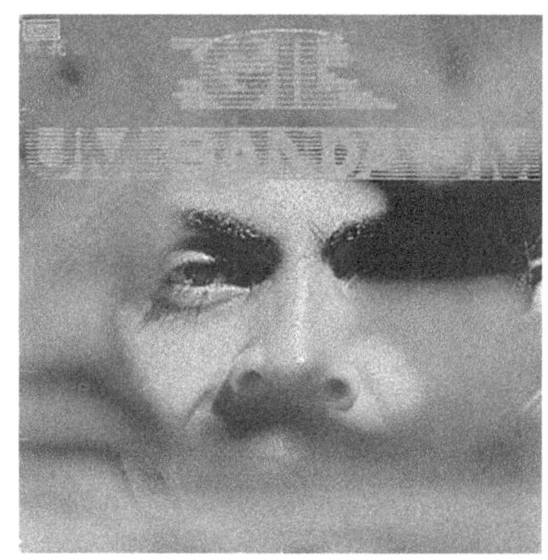

SIDE A
1. Banda Um (Gilberto Gil)
2. Afoxé É (Gilberto Gil)
3. Metáfora (Gilberto Gil)
4. Deixar Você (Gilberto Gil)
5. Pula Caminha (Marino Pinto, Manezinho Araújo)

SIDE B
1. Andar Com Fé (Gilberto Gil)
2. Drão (Gilberto Gil)
3. Esotérico (Gilberto Gil)
4. Menina do Sonho (Gilberto Gil)
5. Ê Menina (João Donato, Guarabyra)
6. Nossa (Gilberto Gil)

**1983
EXTRA**

Label: WEA — BR 36.198
Producer: Liminha

SIDE A

1. Extra (Gilberto Gil)
2. E Lá Poeira (Gilberto Gil, Banda Um)
3. Mar de Copacabana (Gilberto Gil)
4. A Linha E O Linho (Gilberto Gil)
5. Preciso de Você (Gilberto Gil) Featuring: Nara Gil

SIDE B

1. Punk da Periferia (Gilberto Gil)
2. Funk-se Quem Puder (Gilberto Gil)
3. Dono do Pedaço (Gilberto Gil, Waly Salomão, Antônio Cícero)
4. Lady Neyde (Gilberto Gil, Antônio Risério)
5. O Veado (Gilberto Gil)

1984
RAÇA HUMANA

Label: WEA — BR 36.201
Producer: Liminha

SIDE A
1. Extra II (O Rock do Segurança) (Gilberto Gil)
2. Feliz Por Um Triz (Gilberto Gil)
3. Pessoa Nefasta (Gilberto Gil)
4. Tempo Rei (Gilberto Gil)

SIDE B
1. Vamos Fugir (Gilberto Gil, Liminha)
2. A Mão da Limpeza (Gilberto Gil)
3. Índigo Blue (Gilberto Gil)
4. Vem Morena (Luiz Gonzaga, Zé Dantas)
5. Raça Humana (Gilberto Gil)

1985
DIA DORIM NOITE NEON

Label: WEA — BR 36.207
Producer: Liminha

SIDE A

1. Minha Ideologia Minha Religião (Gilberto Gil)
2. Nos Barracos da Cidade (Gilberto Gil, Liminha)
Barracos (Liminha, Gilberto Gil)
3. Roque Santeiro o Rock (Gilberto Gil)
4. Seu Olhar (Gilberto Gil)
5. Febril (Gilberto Gil)
6. Touche Pas a Mon Pote (Gilberto Gil)

SIDE B

1. Logos Versus Logo (Gilberto Gil)
2. Oração Pela Libertação da África do Sul (Gilberto Gil)
3. Clichê do Clichê (Gilberto Gil, Vinícius Cantuária)
4. Casinha Feliz (Gilberto Gil)
5. Duas Luas (Jorge Mautner)

1987
SOY LOCO POR TI, AMÉRICA

Label: WEA — 254 986-1
Producer: Liminha

SIDE A
1. Aquele Abraço (Gilberto Gil)
2. Vida (Roger Kedyh, Maria Juçá)
3. Mamma (Gilberto Gil)
4. Soy Loco Por Ti, América (Gilberto Gil, Capinan)

SIDE B
1. Babá Alapalá (Gilberto Gil)
2. Jubiabá (Gilberto Gil)
3. Mar de Copacabana (Gilberto Gil)
4. Mardi Dix Mars (Gilberto Gil)

1987
AO VIVO EM TOKYO

Label: Geleia Geral — 2202546042

SIDE A

1. Nos Barracos da Cidade (Gilberto Gil, Liminha)
2. Vamos Fugir (Gilberto Gil, Liminha)
3. Aquele Abraço (Gilberto Gil)
4. Oriente (Gilberto Gil)
5. Flora (Gilberto Gil)

SIDE B

1. Sarará Miolo (Gilberto Gil)
2. Banda Um (Gilberto Gil)
3. Touche Pas a Mon Pote (Gilberto Gil)
4. Toda Menina Baiana (Gilberto Gil)
5. Não Chore Mais (No Woman, No Cry) (Vincent Ford, Adapt. Gilberto Gil)

1987
GILBERTO GIL
EM CONCERTO

Label: Geleia Geral — 670.9001
Producer: Liminha
Recorded at the Municipal Theater
and Copacabana Palace, 1986

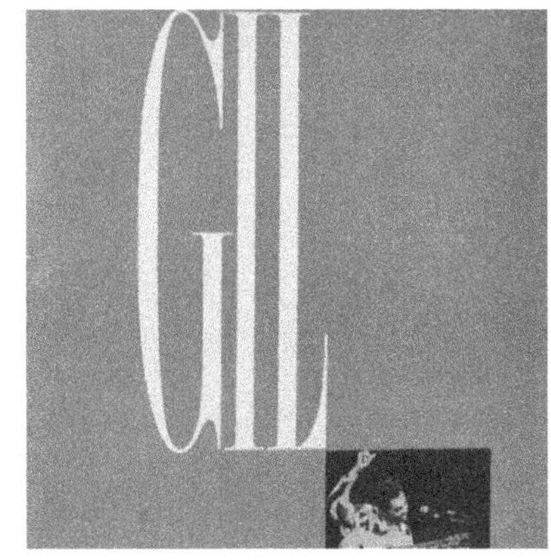

SIDE A

1. Eu Vim da Bahia (Gilberto Gil)
2. Procissão (Gilberto Gil)
3. Domingo No Parque (Gilberto Gil)
4. Soy Loco Por Ti, América (Gilberto Gil, Capinan)
5. Mamma (Gilberto Gil)

SIDE B

1. Cores Vivas (Gilberto Gil)
2. Só Chamei Porque Te Amo (I Just Called To Say I Love You)
(Stevie Wonder, Adapt. Gilberto Gil)
3. Filhos de Gandhi (Gilberto Gil)
4. Palco (Gilberto Gil)

1987
UM TREM PARA AS ESTRELAS
TRILHA SONORA DO FILME

Label: Globo — 402.0002
Producer: Liminha
Soundtrack of the film by
Cacá Diegues

SIDE A

1. Pra Fazer o Sol Nascer (Gilberto Gil) Singers: Gilberto Gil
2. Copacabana Funk (Gilberto Gil)
3. Pagode da Santinha (Anilton da Costa, Douglas Sarão Bezerra)
Singers: Grupo Guiné
4. Camila (Gilberto Gil)
5. Milagre na Favela (Gilberto Gil)
6. A Santa na Cruz (Gilberto Gil)

SIDE B

1. Um Trem Para As Estrelas (Cazuza, Gilberto Gil)
Singers: Gilberto Gil e Cazuza
2. A Existência do Sol (Gilberto Gil)
3. Romance do Cabo Com a Santa (Gilberto Gil)
4. Agonia de Drime (Gilberto Gil)
5. Morte de Drime (Gilberto Gil)
6. Noite de Amor (Gilberto Gil)
7. Fox no Mercado (Gilberto Gil)

1989
O ETERNO DEUS MU DANÇA

Label: Warner — 670.8059
Producers: Celso Fonseca
and Vitor Farias

SIDE A
1. O Eterno Deus Mu Dança (Gilberto Gil, Celso Fonseca)
Featuring: Ed Motta
2. Mulher de Coronel (Gilberto Gil)
3. De Bob Dylan a Bob Marley Um Samba Provocação (Gilberto Gil)
4. Cada Tempo Em Seu Lugar (Gilberto Gil)
5. Baticum (Chico Buarque, Gilberto Gil) Featuring: Chico Buarque

SIDE B
1. Do Japão (Gilberto Gil)
2. Mon Thiers Monde (Gilberto Gil)
3. Amarra o Teu Arado a Uma Estrela (Gilberto Gil)
4. Réquiem Pra Mãe Menininha do Gantois (Gilberto Gil)
5. Toda Saudade (Gilberto Gil)

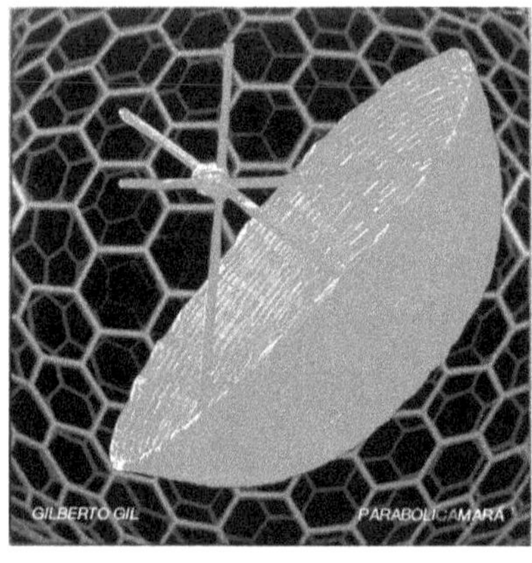

1991
PARABOLICAMARÁ

Label: Warner — 01397
Producer: Liminha

SIDE A

1. Madalena (Entra Em Beco, Sai Em Beco) (Isidoro, Adpt. Gilberto Gil)
2. Parabolicamará (Gilberto Gil)
3. Um Sonho (Gilberto Gil)
4. Buda Nagô (Gilberto Gil)
Featuring: Nana Caymmi
5. Serafim (Gilberto Gil)

SIDE B

1. Quero Ser Teu Funk (Gilberto Gil, Dé, Liminha)
2. Neve na Bahia (Gilberto Gil)
3. Yá Olokum (Mônica Millet, Fred Vieira)
4. O Fim da História (Gilberto Gil)
5. De Onde Vem O Baião (Gilberto Gil)

1992
TROPICÁLIA 2

Label: Polygram — 518 178-1
Producer: Liminha

SIDE A
1. Haiti (Gilberto Gil, Caetano Veloso)
2. Cinema Novo (Gilberto Gil, Caetano Veloso)
3. Nossa Gente (Avisa Lá) (Roque Carvalho)
4. Rap Popcreto (Caetano Veloso)
5. Wait Until Tomorrow (Jimi Hendrix)
6. Tradição (Gilberto Gil)

SIDE B
1. As Coisas (Gilberto Gil, Arnaldo Antunes)
2. Aboio (Caetano Veloso)
3. Dada (Caetano Veloso, Gilberto Gil)
4. Cada Macaco No Seu Galho (Riachão)
5. Baião Atemporal (Gilberto Gil)
6. Desde Que O Samba É Samba (Caetano Veloso)

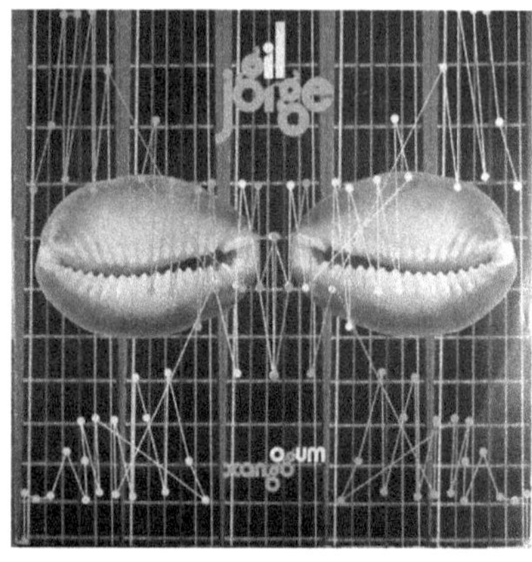

1994
UNPLUGGED

Label: Warner — 995323-2
Recorded live on the program
Acústico MTV

1. A Novidade (Herbert Vianna, Bi Ribeiro, João Barone, Gilberto Gil)
2. Tenho Sede (Dominguinhos, Anastácia)
3. Refazenda (Gilberto Gil)
4. Realce (Gilberto Gil)
5. Esotérico (Gilberto Gil)
6. Drão (Gilberto Gil)
7. A Paz (João Donato, Gilberto Gil)
8. Beira Mar (Gilberto Gil, Caetano Veloso)
9. Sampa (Caetano Veloso)
10. Parabolicamará (Gilberto Gil)
11. Tempo Rei (Gilberto Gil)
12. Expresso 2222 (Gilberto Gil)
13. Aquele Abraço (Gilberto Gil)
14. Palco (Gilberto Gil)
15. Toda Menina Baiana (Gilberto Gil)
16. Sítio do Pica-Pau Amarelo (Gilberto Gil)

1997
QUANTA
(DISCO 1)

Label: Warner — 063013033-2
Producer: Liminha

1. Quanta (Gilberto Gil)
Featuring: Milton Nascimento
2. Ciência e Arte (Cartola, Carlos Cachaça)
3. Estrela (Gilberto Gil)
4. Dança De Shiva (Gilberto Gil)
5. Vendedor de Caranguejo (Gordurinha)
6. Água Benta (Gilberto Gil)
7. Chiquinho Azevedo (Gilberto Gil)
8. Pílula De Alho (Gilberto Gil)
9. Opachorô (Gilberto Gil)
10. Graça Divina (Gilberto Gil)
11. Pela Internet (Gilberto Gil)
12. Guerra Santa (Gilberto Gil)
13. Objeto Sim, Objeto Não (Gilberto Gil)

1997
QUANTA
(DISCO 2)

Label: Warner — 063013033-2
Producer: Liminha

1. A Ciência Em Si (Gilberto Gil, Arnaldo Antunes)
2. Átimo De Pó (Gilberto Gil/Carlos Rennó)
3. Labirinto (Jorge Mautner, Nelson Jacobina)
4. Fogo Líquido (Gilberto Gil)
5. Pop Wu Wei (Gilberto Gil)
6. O Lugar Do Nosso Amor (Gilberto Gil)
7. De Ouro E Marfim (Gilberto Gil)
8. Sala Do Som (Gilberto Gil)
9. Um Abraço No João (Gilberto Gil)
10. O Mar E O Lago (Gilberto Gil)
11. La Lune de Gorée (Gilberto Gil, Capinan)
12. Nova (Gilberto Gil, Moreno Veloso)
13. Objeto Ainda Menos Identificado (Lucas Santtana, Moreno Veloso)

1998
QUANTA GENTE VEIO VER

Label: Warner — 398422067-2
Recorded live at Teatro João Caetano - Rio de Janeiro, on August 13 and 14, 1997

1. Introdução (Sandrão)
2. Palco (Gilberto Gil)
3. Is This Love (Bob Marley)
4. Stir It Up (Bob Marley)
5. Refavela (Gilberto Gil)
6. Vendedor de Caranguejo (Gordurinha)
7. Quanta (Gilberto Gil)
8. Estrela (Gilberto Gil)
9. Pela Internet (Gilberto Gil)
10. Cérebro Eletrônico (Gilberto Gil)
11. Opachorô (Gilberto Gil)
12. Copacabana (João de Barro, Alberto Ribeiro)
13. A Novidade (Herbert Vianna, Bi Ribeiro, João Barone, Gilberto Gil)
14. O Ghandi (Antônio do Caixão)
15. De Ouro E Marfim (Gilberto Gil)
16. Doce De Carnaval (Candy All) (Gilberto Gil)
17. Lamento De Carnaval (Gilberto Gil) Featuring: Lulu Santos
18. Pretinha (Gilberto Gil, Kátia Falcão, João Donato)

1998
CIDADE DE SALVADOR
(DISCO 1)

Label: Polygram — 538 592-2
Research: Marcelo Fróes
Collection of rare or unreleased
recordings of songs recorded in
1973 and 1974

1. Meio de Campo (Gilberto Gil)
2. Eu Só Quero Um Xodó (Dominguinhos, Anastácia)
3. Edyth Cooper (Gilberto Gil)
4. Umeboshi (Gilberto Gil)
5. Essa É Pra Tocar no Rádio (Gilberto Gil)
6. Tradição (Gilberto Gil)
7. Minha Nega na Janela (Germano Mathias, Doca)
8. Ó, Maria (Gilberto Gil)
9. A Última Valsa (Gilberto Gil, Rogério Duarte)
10. Ladeira da Preguiça (Gilberto Gil)
11. Rainha do Mar (Dorival Caymmi)
12. Iansã (Gilberto Gil, Caetano Veloso)
13. Doente, Morena (Duda Machado, Gilberto Gil)

1998
CIDADE DE SALVADOR
(DISCO 2)

Label: Polygram — 538 592-2
Research: Marcelo Fróes
Collection of rare or unreleased
recordings of songs recorded in
1973 and 1974

1. Cidade Do Salvador (Gilberto Gil)
2. Imbalança (Luiz Gonzaga, Zé Dantas)
3. Duplo Sentido (Gilberto Gil)
4. Preciso Aprender A Só Ser (Gilberto Gil)
5. Maracatu Atômico (Jorge Mautner, Nelson Jacobina)
6. Maracatu Atômico (Jorge Mautner, Nelson Jacobina)
7. Todo Dia É Dia D (Carlos Pinto, Torquato Neto)
8. Esses Moços (Pobres Moços) (Lupicínio Rodrigues)
9. Meditação (Gilberto Gil)
10. Pocalipi (versão 1) (Gilberto Gil)
11. Poçalipi (versão 2) (Gilberto Gil)
12. Maracatu Atômico (Jorge Mautner, Nelson Jacobina)

1998
O VIRAMUNDO
AO VIVO 1972-1976

Label: Polygram — 538 589-2
Research: Marcelo Fróes
A collection of live recordings
made between 1972 and 1976

1. Cada Macaco No Seu Galho (Riachão)
2. Ele e Eu (Gilberto Gil)
3. Back In Bahia (Gilberto Gil)
4. Expresso 2222 (Gilberto Gil)
5. Objeto Sim, Objeto Não (Gilberto Gil)
6. Oriente (Gilberto Gil)
7. Procissão (Gilberto Gil)
8. Domingo No Parque (Gilberto Gil)
9. O Bom Jogador (Gilberto Gil)
10. Brand New Dream (Gilberto Gil)
11. Viramundo (Gilberto Gil, Capinan)
12. Baby Hippie (Jorge Mautner)
13. Músico Simples (Gilberto Gil)
14. Lamento Sertanejo (Dominguinhos, Gilberto Gil)
15. Planeta Dos Macacos (Jorge Mautner, Jards Macalé)
16. Gaivota (Gilberto Gil)
17. Queremos Saber (Gilberto Gil)
18. A Sociedade Afluente (Gilberto Gil)
19. Filhos de Gandhi (Gilberto Gil)

1998
SATISFAÇÃO

Label: Polygram — R 765.087 L
Research: Marcelo Fróes
A collection of unreleased and rare
songs recorded between 1976
and 1977

1. Ninguém Segura Este País (Gilberto Gil)
2. Satisfação (Gilberto Gil)
3. Sentimentos (Mijinha); Ladeira da Preguiça (Gilberto Gil)
4. Há, Há, Há (Gilberto Gil) Featuring: Chico Batera, A Cozinha Manteca
5. Tiu, Ru, Ru (Cat Stevens, Gilberto Gil) Featuring: Chico Batera,
A Cozinha Manteca
6. A Bruxa De Mentira (João Donato, Gilberto Gil) Featuring: João Donato
7. Chuck Berry Fields Forever (Gilberto Gil) Featuring: Doces Bárbaros
8. Sarará Miolo (Gilberto Gil). Featuring: Nara Leão
9. É (Gilberto Gil)
10. Músico Simples (Gilberto Gil)
11. Sala Do Som (Gilberto Gil)
1. Brazil Very Happy Band (Gilberto Gil) Featuring: Brazil Very Happy Band
13. Tipo África (P. Santana, R. Silva, C. Teixeira, R. Sabino, D. Correia, Julinho,
Chocolate) Featuring: Brazil Very Happy Band
14. Ojú Obá (Edil Pacheco, Paulo César Pinheiro)

1998
COPACABANA MON AMOUR
TRILHA SONORA DO FILME

Label: Polygram — 012 919-2
Soundtrack of the film
by Rogério Sganzerla (1971),
previously unpublished

1. Diga A Ela (1ª Versão) (Gilberto Gil)
2. Mr. Sganzerla (Gilberto Gil)
3. Blind Faith (Gilberto Gil)
4. Yeh Yeh Yah Yah (Gilberto Gil)
5. Tomorrow Vai Ser Bacana (Gilberto Gil)
6. Diga A Ela (2ª Versão) (Gilberto Gil)

1998
O SOL DE OSLO

Label: Pau Brasil — PB 014
Recorded at Rainbow Studio,
Oslo, Norway

1. Tatá Engenho Novo (Tradicional)
2. Mana (Tradicional)
3. Dezessete Na Corrente (Edgard Ferreira, Manoel Firmino Alves)
4. Xote (Gilberto Gil, Rodolfo Stroeter)
5. Eu Te Dei Meu Ané (Gilberto Gil, Marlui Miranda)
6. Kaô (Gilberto Gil, Rodolfo Stroeter)
7. Ciranda (Gilberto Gil, Moacir Santos)
8. Rep (Gilberto Gil)
9. Onde O Xaxado Tá (Gilberto Gil, Rodolfo Stroeter)
10. Língua do P (Gilberto Gil)
11. A Santinha Lá Da Serra (Moacir Santos, Vinicius de Moraes)
12. Ai Baiano (Tradicional)
13. Bastiana (Marlui Miranda)
14. Oslodum (Gilberto Gil)

2000
GIL E MILTON

Label: Warner — 8579385738-2
Producer: Guto Graça Mello
Artists: Gilberto Gil and
Milton Nascimento

1. Sebastian (Gilberto Gil, Milton Nascimento)
2. Duas Sanfonas (Gilberto Gil, Milton Nascimento)
3. Ponta de Areia (Milton Nascimento, Fernando Brant)
4. Bom Dia (Gilberto Gil, Nana Caymmi)
5. Trovoada (Gilberto Gil, Milton Nascimento)
6. Something (George Harrison)
7. Maria (Ary Barroso, Luis Peixoto)
8. Lar Hospitalar (Milton Nascimento, Gilberto Gil)
9. Yo Vengo A Ofrecer Mi Corazón (Fito Paez)
10. Dora (Dorival Caymmi)
11. Xica da Silva (Jorge Ben Jor)
12. Canção do Sal (Milton Nascimento)
13. Dinamarca (Milton Nascimento, Gilberto Gil)
14. Palco (Gilberto Gil)
15. Baião da Garoa (Luiz Gonzaga, Hervé Cordovil)

2000

**AS CANÇÕES DE
EU TU ELES**

Label: Warner — 857382768-2
Producer: Gilberto Gil
Soundtrack of the film
by Andrucha Waddington

1. Óia Eu Aqui de Novo (Antônio Barros)
2. Baião da Penha (Guio de Morais, David Nasser)
3. Esperando Na Janela (Targino Gondim, Manuca Almeida,
Raimundinho do Acordeon)
4. Juazeiro (Luiz Gonzaga, Humberto Teixeira)
5. Último Pau-de-Arara (Venâncio, Corumba, José Guimarães)
6. Asa Branca (Luiz Gonzaga, Humberto Teixeira)
7. Qui Nem Jiló (Luiz Gonzaga, Humberto Teixeira)
8. Assum Preto (Luiz Gonzaga, Humberto Teixeira)
9. Pau-de-Arara (Guio de Morais, Luiz Gonzaga)
10. A Volta da Asa Branca (Luiz Gonzaga, Zé Dantas)
11. O Amor Daqui Dc Casa (Gilberto Gil)
12. As Pegadas Do Amor (Gilberto Gil)
13. Lamento Sertanejo (Dominguinhos, Gilberto Gil)
14. Casinha Feliz (Gilberto Gil)

2001
SÃO JOÃO AO VIVO

Label: Warner — 857385964-2
Producer: Gilberto Gil
Recorded live at Vila Funchal,
São Paulo, on June 11th, 2000

1. Olha Pro Céu (Luiz Gonzaga, José Fernandes)
2. Óia Eu Aqui de Novo (Antônio Barros)
3. Asa Branca (Luiz Gonzaga, Humberto Teixeira)
4. Baião da Penha (Guio de Morais, David Nasser)
5. Qui Nem Jiló (Luiz Gonzaga, Humberto Teixeira)
6. Baião (Luiz Gonzaga, Humberto Teixeira); De Onde Vem O Baião (Gilberto Gil)
7. Lamento Sertanejo (Dominguinhos, Gilberto Gil)
8. Cajuína (Caetano Veloso); Refazenda (Gilberto Gil)
9. Pau-de-Arara (Guio de Morais, Luiz Gonzaga)
10. Respeita Januário (Luiz Gonzaga, Humberto Teixeira)
11. O Xote das Meninas (Luiz Gonzaga, Zé Dantas)
12. Eu Só Quero Um Xodó (Dominguinhos, Anastácia)
13. Vem Morena (Luiz Gonzaga, Zé Dantas)
14. Esperando Na Janela (Targino Gondim, Manuca Almeida, Raimundinho do Acordeon)
15. Último Pau-de-Arara (Venâncio, Corumba, José Guimarães)
16. Madalena (Entra Em Beco, Sai Em Beco) (Isidoro, Adpt. Gilberto Gil)
17. Toda Menina Baiana (Gilberto Gil)
18. Na Casa Dela (Gilberto Gil)

2002
KAYA N'GAN DAYA

Label: Warner — 092742166-2
Producer: Tom Capone

1. Buffalo Soldier (Bob Marley, Noel George Williams)
2. One Drop (Bob Marley)
3. Waiting In Vain (Bob Marley)
4. Table Tennis Table (Gilberto Gil)
5. Three Little Birds (Bob Marley)
6. Não Chore Mais (No Woman, No Cry) (Vincent Ford, Adapt. Gilberto Gil)
Featuring: Os Paralamas do Sucesso
7. Positive Vibration (Vincent Ford)
8. Could You Be Loved (Bob Marley) Featuring: Henrique Portugal, Samuel Rosa
9. Kaya N'gan Daya (Kaya) (Bob Marley, Adapt. Gilberto Gil)
10. Rebel Music (3 O'Clock Road Block) (Aston Barrett, Hugh Peart)
11. Them Bellyfull (But We Hungry) (Carlton Barrett, Lecon Cogill)
Featuring: Os Paralamas do Sucesso
12. Tempo Só (Time Will Tell) (Bob Marley, Adapt. Gilberto Gil)
13. Easy Skankin' (Bob Marley)
14. Turn Your Lights Down Low (Bob Marley)
15. Eleve-se Alto ao Céu (Lively Up Yourself) (Bob Marley, Adapt. Gilberto Gil)
16. Lick Samba (Bob Marley)

2002
TO BE ALIVE IS GOOD
(ANOS 80)

Label: Warner — 092747427-2
Research: Marcelo Fróes
A collection of unreleased and rare songs recorded in the 1980s

1. It's Good To Be Alive (Versão 1985) (Gilberto Gil)
2. Titicaca (Gilberto Gil)
3. Afoxé Badauê (Paulinho Camafeu)
4. Corações À Mil (Gilberto Gil)
5. TV Punk (Gilberto Gil)
6. Oxalá (Cesta Cheia da Sexta) (Moraes Moreira, Paulo Leminski)
7. Pílula De Alho (Gilberto Gil)
8. Estrela (Gilberto Gil)
9. Quatro Modos (Gilberto Gil)
10. Música Moderna (Gilberto Gil)
11. Serafim (Gilberto Gil)
12. Noite De Lua Cheia (Gilberto Gil)
13. Todo Dia De Manhã (Gilberto Gil)
14. Punk da Periferia (Gilberto Gil)
15. Por Que Alguém Tem Inveja de Você (Gilberto Gil)
16. Sítio do Pica-Pau Amarelo (Versão 1985) (Gilberto Gil)
17. Pode, Waldir? (Gilberto Gil)

2002

IT'S GOOD TO BE ALIVE
(ANOS 90)

Label: Warner — 092747427-2
Research: Marcelo Fróes
A collection of unreleased and rare
songs recorded in the 1990s

1. It's Good To Be Alive (Versão 1996) (Gilberto Gil)

2. Língua do P (Gilberto Gil)

3. Terra 90 (Gilberto Gil)

4. Treze De Dezembro (Luiz Gonzaga, Zé Dantas, Gilberto Gil)

5. Padroeiro do Brasil (Irany de Oliveira, Ari Monteiro)

6. Chiquinho Azevedo (Gilberto Gil)

7. A Faca E O Queijo (Gilberto Gil)

8. Poema Aritimimético (Gilberto Gil)

9. Afrolodumultimídia (Lucas Santtana, Quito Ribeiro)

10. Você e Você (Gilberto Gil)

11. Mãe Solteira (Wilson Batista, Jorge de Castro)

12. Pelo Telefone (Donga, Mauro de Almeida) Live

13. Pela Internet (Gilberto Gil) Live

14. Cérebro Eletrônico (Gilberto Gil) Live

15. O Mar E O Lago (Gilberto Gil) Live

16. Buda Nagô (Gilberto Gil) Live

17. Aquele Abraço (Gilberto Gil) Live

2002
SALVADOR 1962-1963

Label: Warner — 092747212-2
Research: Marcelo Fróes
Songs released between 1962 and
1963 in 78rpm

1. Povo Petroleiro (Everaldo Guedes)
2. Coça, Coça, Lacerdinha (Everaldo Guedes)
3. Serenata Em Teleco-Teco (Gilberto Gil)
4. Maria Tristeza (Gilberto Gil)
5. Vontade De Amar (Gilberto Gil)
6. Meu Luar, Minhas Canções (Gilberto Gil)
7. Amor de Carnaval (Gilberto Gil)
8. Vem Colombina (Sivan Castelo Neto, Jorge Santos)

2003
KAYA N'GAN DAYA AO VIVO

Label: Globo Warner — 3098-2
Producer: Tom Capone

1. Eleve-se Alto ao Céu (Lively Up Yourself) (Bob Marley, Adapt. Gilberto Gil)
2. Não Chore Mais (No Woman, No Cry) (Vincent Ford, Adapt. Gilberto Gil)
3. Kaya N'gan Daya (Kaya) (Bob Marley, Adapt. Gilberto Gil)
4. Rebel Music (3 O'Clock Road Block) (Aston Barrett, Hugh Peart)
5. Vamos Fugir (Gilberto Gil, Liminha)
6. Them Bellyfull (But We Hungry) (Carlton Barrett, Lecon Cogill)
7. A Novidade (Herbert Vianna, Bi Ribeiro, João Barone, Gilberto Gil)
8. Waiting In Vain (Bob Marley)
9. Three Little Birds (Bob Marley)
10. Garota de Ipanema (Tom Jobim, Vinicius de Moraes)
11. Extra (Gilberto Gil)
12. Nos Barracos da Cidade (Gilberto Gil, Liminha)
13. Is This Love (Bob Marley)
14. Could You Be Loved (Bob Marley)
15. Alagados (Herbert Vianna, Bi Ribeiro, João Barone)
16. Sítio do Pica-Pau Amarelo (Gilberto Gil)
17. Esperando Na Janela (Targino Gondim, Manuca Almeida, Raimundinho do Acordeon)

2004
ELETRACÚSTICO

Label: Warner — 5050467589827
Producer: Liminha
Recorded live at Canecão,
September 2004

1. Refavela (Gilberto Gil)
2. Andar Com Fé (Gilberto Gil)
3. Chuck Berry Fields Forever (Gilberto Gil)
4. Cambalache (Enrique Santos Discépolo)
5. Imagine (John Lennon)
6. A Rita (Chico Buarque)
7. A Linha E O Linho (Gilberto Gil)
8. Aquele Abraço (Gilberto Gil)
9. Maracatu Atômico (Jorge Mautner, Nelson Jacobina)
10. Se Eu Quiser Falar Com Deus (Gilberto Gil)
11. La Lune de Gorée (Gilberto Gil, Capinan)
12. Three Little Birds (Bob Marley)
13. Guerra Santa (Gilberto Gil)
14. Soy Loco Por Ti, América (Gilberto Gil, Capinan)

2006
GIL LUMINOSO
(VOZ E VIOLÃO)

Label: Biscoito Fino — BF 665
Producer: Bené Fonteles

1. Preciso Aprender A Só Ser (Gilberto Gil)
2. Aqui e Agora (Gilberto Gil)
3. Copo Vazio (Gilberto Gil)
4. Retiros Espirituais (Gilberto Gil)
5. O Seu Amor (Gilberto Gil)
6. Tempo Rei (Gilberto Gil)
7. O Som da Pessoa (Gilberto Gil, Bené Fonteles)
8. Cérebro Eletrônico (Gilberto Gil)
9. Raça Humana (Gilberto Gil)
10. Você E Eu (Gilberto Gil)
11. Super-Homem (A Canção) (Gilberto Gil)
12. Rebento (Gilberto Gil)
13. Metáfora (Gilberto Gil)
14. Meditação (Gilberto Gil)
15. O Compositor Me Disse (Gilberto Gil)

2008
BANDA LARGA CORDEL

Label: Warner — 2564695033
Producer: Liminha

1. Despedida de Solteira (Gilberto Gil)
2. Os Pais (Jorge Mautner, Gilberto Gil)
3. Não Grude, Não (Gilberto Gil)
4. Formosa (Baden Powell, Vinicius de Moraes)
5. Samba de Los Angeles (Gilberto Gil)
6. La Renaissance Africaine (Gilberto Gil)
7. Olho Mágico (Gilberto Gil)
8. Não Tenho Medo da Morte (Gilberto Gil)
9. Amor de Carnaval (Gilberto Gil)
10. Gueixa No Tatame (Gilberto Gil)
11. A Faca E O Queijo (Gilberto Gil)
12. Outros Viram (Jorge Mautner, Gilberto Gil)
13. Canô (Gilberto Gil)
14. Máquina de Ritmo (Gilberto Gil)
15. Banda Larga Cordel (Gilberto Gil)
16. O Oco do Mundo (Gilberto Gil)

2008
BANDA DOIS

Label: Warner — 2564684258
Recorded at Bradesco Theater,
São Paulo, on September 28th
and 29th, 2009

1. Esotérico (Gilberto Gil)
2. A Linha E O Linho (Gilberto Gil)
3. Super-Homem (A Canção) (Gilberto Gil)
4. Saudade da Bahia (Dorival Caymmi)
5. Chiclete Com Banana (Gordurinha, Almira Castilho)
6. Das Duas, Uma (Gilberto Gil)
7. Quatro Coisas (Gilberto Gil)
8. Amor Até O Fim (Gilberto Gil) Featuring: Maria Rita
9. Lamento Sertanejo (Dominguinhos, Gilberto Gil)
10. O Rouxinol (Gilberto Gil, Jorge Mautner)
11. Refazenda (Gilberto Gil)
12. Banda Um (Gilberto Gil)
13. La Renaissance Africaine (Gilberto Gil)
14. Refavela (Gilberto Gil)
15. Babá Alapalá (Gilberto Gil)
16. Expresso 2222 (Gilberto Gil)

2010
FÉ NA FESTA

Label: Universal — 60252741055
Producer: Sergio Chiavazzolli

1. Fé Na Festa (Gilberto Gil)
2. O Livre-Atirador e a Pegadora (Gilberto Gil)
3. Assim, Sim (Gilberto Gil)
4. Estrela Azul do Céu (Gilberto Gil)
5. Marmundo (Gilberto Gil)
6. Vinte E Seis (Gilberto Gil)
7. Não Tenho Medo da Vida (Gilberto Gil)
8. Norte da Saudade (Perinho Santana, Moacir Albuquerque, Gilberto Gil)
9. Maria Minha (Targino Gondim, Eliezer Setton)
10. Aprendi Com O Rei (João Silva)
11. Dança da Moda (Luiz Gonzaga, Zé Dantas)
12. São João Carioca (Gilberto Gil, Nando Cordel)
13. Lá Vem Ela (Gilberto Gil, Vanessa da Mata)

2010
FÉ NA FESTA AO VIVO

Label: Universal — 60252756740

1. Fé Na Festa (Gilberto Gil)
2. Dança da Moda (Luiz Gonzaga, Zé Dantas)
3. Assim, Sim (Gilberto Gil)
4. Óia Eu Aqui de Novo (Antônio Barros)
5. Respeita Januário (Luiz Gonzaga, Humberto Teixeira); O Xote das Meninas (Luiz Gonzaga, Zé Dantas); Eu Só Quero Um Xodó (Dominguinhos, Anastácia)
6. Lamento Sertanejo (Dominguinhos, Gilberto Gil)
7. Um Riacho, Um Caminho (Gilberto Gil, Dominguinhos)
8. Juazeiro (Luiz Gonzaga, Humberto Teixeira)
9. Estrela Azul do Céu (Gilberto Gil)
10. Aprendi Com O Rei (João Silva)
11. O Livre Atirador e a Pegadora (Gilberto Gil)
12. Qui Nem Jiló (Luiz Gonzaga, Humberto Teixeira); Expresso 2222 (Gilberto Gil)
13. O Casamento da Raposa (Gerson Filho)
14. Olha Pro Céu (Luiz Gonzaga, José Fernandes)
15. Esperando Na Janela (Targino Gondim, Manuca Almeida, Raimundinho do Acordeon)

2011

GIL + 10 CONVIDA

Label: Go 2 Music
Recorded live at Espaço Tom Jobim (Rio de Janeiro)

1. Palco (Gilberto Gil)
2. A Linha E O Linho (Gilberto Gil) Featuring: Lenine
3. Aquele Abraço (Gilberto Gil) Featuring: Zeca Pagodinho
4. Extra II (O Rock do Segurança) (Gilberto Gil) Featuring: Erasmo Carlos
5. Torpedo (Ana Carolina, Mombaça, Gilberto Gil) Featuring: Ana Carolina
6. Andar Com Fé (Gilberto Gil); Vida (Roger Kedyh, Maria Juçá)
Featuring: Preta Gil
7. Cálice (Chico Buarque, Gilberto Gil) Featuring: Milton Nascimento
8. Lamento Sertanejo (Dominguinhos, Gilberto Gil)
Featuring: Milton Nascimento, Maria Gadú
9. Acreditar (Dona Ivone Lara, Délcio Carvalho) Featuring: Dona Ivone Lara
10. Alguém Me Avisou (Dona Ivone Lara) Featuring: Dona Ivone Lara
11. Deixar Você (Gilberto Gil) Featuring: Mart'nália
12. A Novidade (Herbert Vianna, Bi Ribeiro, João Barone, Gilberto Gil)
Featuring: Os Paralamas do Sucesso
13. Essa É Pra Tocar no Rádio (Gilberto Gil)

2012

CONCERTO DE CORDAS
E MÁQUINAS DE RITMO

Label: Biscoito Fino — BF 196-2
Arrangements: Jacques More-
lenbaum
Recorded live at the Theatro
Municipal (Rio de Janeiro),
on May 28th, 2012

1. Máquina de Ritmo (Gilberto Gil)
2. Eu Vim da Bahia (Gilberto Gil)
3. Estrela (Gilberto Gil)
4. Quanta (Gilberto Gil)
5. Futurível (Gilberto Gil)
6. Eu Descobri (Gilberto Gil)
7. Outra Vez (Tom Jobim)
8. Não Tenho Medo da Morte (Gilberto Gil)
9. Juazeiro (Luiz Gonzaga, Humberto Teixeira)
10. Tres Palabras (Osvaldo Farrés)
11. La Renaissance Africaine (Gilberto Gil)
12. Panis Et Circenses (Caetano Veloso, Gilberto Gil)
13. Oriente (Gilberto Gil)
14. Andar Com Fé (Gilberto Gil)
15. Domingo No Parque (Gilberto Gil)

2014

GILBERTO GIL E GAL COSTA
AO VIVO EM LONDRES 1971

Label: Discobertas — 332161
Research: Marcelo Fróes
Recorded live on November 26, 1971, at the Student Centre, City University London (England)

1. Coração Vagabundo (Caetano Veloso)
2. Sai do Sereno (Onildo Almeida)
3. Vapor Barato (Jards Macalé, Waly Salomão)
4. Como Dois E Dois (Caetano Veloso)
5. Dê Um Rolê (Moraes Moreira, Galvão)
6. Maria Bethânia (Caetano Veloso)
Bota A Mão Nas Cadeiras (Tradicional)
7. Chuva, Suor E Cerveja (Caetano Veloso)
8. Falsa Baiana (Geraldo Pereira)
9. Acauã (Zé Dantas)
10. Procissão (Gilberto Gil)
11. Brand New Dream (Gilberto Gil)
12. Expresso 2222 (Gilberto Gil)
13. Aquele Abraço (Gilberto Gil)
14. Sgt. Pepper's Lonely Hearts Club Band (John Lennon, Paul McCartney)
15. One O'Clock Last Morning 20th April 1970 (Gilberto Gil)
16. Oriente (Gilberto Gil)
17. Up From The Skies (Jimi Hendrix)
18. Viramundo (Gilberto Gil, Capinan)

2014
GILBERTOS SAMBA

Label: Sony — 88843037532
Producers: Bem Gil
and Moreno Veloso

1. Aos Pés da Cruz (Marino Pinto, Zé da Zilda)
2. Eu Sambo Mesmo (Janet de Almeida)
3. O Pato (Jaime Silva, Neuza Teixeira)
4. Tintim Por Tintim (Haroldo Barbosa, Geraldo Jacques)
5. Desde Que O Samba É Samba (Caetano Veloso)
6. Desafinado (Tom Jobim, Newton Mendonça)
7. Milagre (Dorival Caymmi)
8. Um Abraço No João (Gilberto Gil)
9. Doralice (Dorival Caymmi, Antônio Almeida)
10. Você E Eu (Carlos Lyra, Vinicius de Moraes)
11. Eu Vim da Bahia (Gilberto Gil)
12. Gilbertos (Gilberto Gil)

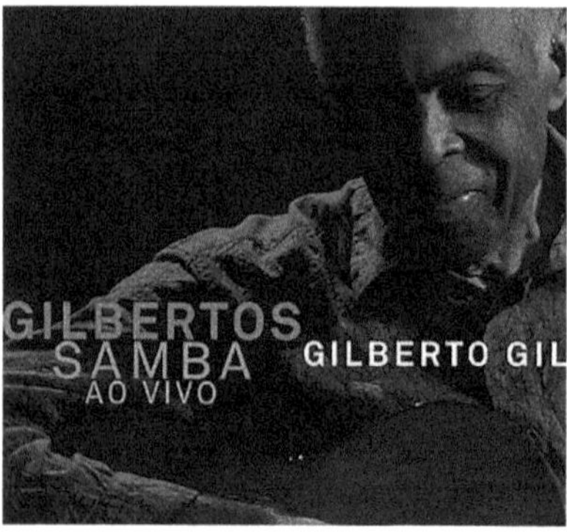

2014
GILBERTOS SAMBA AO VIVO

Label: Warner — 888750350220
Producer: Gilberto Gil

1. Aos Pés da Cruz (Marino Pinto, Zé da Zilda)
2. Você E Eu (Carlos Lyra, Vinicius de Moraes)
3. Tintim Por Tintim (Haroldo Barbosa, Geraldo Jacques)
4. Rosa Morena (Dorival Caymmi)
5. Desde Que O Samba É Samba (Caetano Veloso)
6. Rio Eu Te Amo (Gilberto Gil)
7. O Pato (Jaime Silva, Neuza Teixeira)
8. Doralice (Dorival Caymmi, Antônio Almeida)
9. Um Abraço No João (Gilberto Gil); Gilbertos (Gilberto Gil)
10. Ladeira da Preguiça (Gilberto Gil)
11. Desafinado (Tom Jobim, Newton Mendonça)
12. Máquina de Ritmo (Gilberto Gil)
13. Milagre (Dorival Caymmi)
14. Eu Sambo Mesmo (Janet de Almeida)
15. Mancada (Gilberto Gil); Chiclete Com Banana (Gordurinha, Almira Castilho)
16. Meio de Campo (Gilberto Gil)
17. Eu Vim da Bahia (Gilberto Gil)
18. Aquele Abraço (Gilberto Gil)
19. É Luxo Só (Ary Barroso, Luis Peixoto)

2015
**JORGE MAUTNER E
GILBERTO GIL
O POETA E O ESFOMEADO**

Label: Discobertas — DB-392
Research: Marcelo Fróes
Recorded live at the Palácio das
Convenções do Anehmbi/SP in
March 1987.

1. Positivismo (Noel Rosa, Orestes Barbosa)
2. Marcha Turca (W. A. Mozart)
3. Teu Olhar (Ismael Silva)
4. Casinha Feliz (Gilberto Gil)
5. Você Me Chamou de Nego (Gasolina)
6. A. E. I. O. U. (Lamartine Babo, Noel Rosa); Cores Vivas (Gilberto Gil)
7. Oração Pela Libertação da África do Sul (Gilberto Gil)
8. Vampiro (Jorge Mautner)
9. O Rouxinol (Gilberto Gil, Jorge Mautner)
10. O Filho Predileto de Xangô (Jorge Mautner)
11. Mamma (Gilberto Gil)
12. Maracatu Atômico (Jorge Mautner, Nelson Jacobina)
13. Hino da Figa (Gilberto Gil)

2015

CAETANO E GIL: DOIS AMIGOS, UM SÉCULO DE MÚSICA (DISC 1)

Label: Sony — 88875179222
Live at Multishow TV Channel

1. Back In Bahia (Gilberto Gil)
2. Coração Vagabundo (Caetano Veloso)
3. Tropicália (Caetano Veloso)
4. Marginália II (Gilberto Gil, Torquato Neto)
5. É Luxo Só (Ary Barroso, Luis Peixoto)
6. De Manhã (Caetano Veloso)
7. As Camélias do Quilombo do Lebron (Caetano Veloso, Gilberto Gil)
8. Sampa (Caetano Veloso)
9. Terra (Caetano Veloso)
10. Nine Out Of Ten (Caetano Veloso)
11. Odeio (Caetano Veloso)
12. Tonada de Luna Llena (Simon Diaz)
13. Eu Vim da Bahia (Gilberto Gil)

2015
CAETANO E GIL: DOIS AMIGOS, UM SÉCULO DE MÚSICA (DISC 2)

Label: Sony — 88875179222
Live at Multishow TV Channel

1. Super-Homem (A Canção) (Gilberto Gil)
2. Come Prima (Mario Panzeri, Sandro Taccani, Vincenzo Di Paola)
3. Esotérico (Gilberto Gil)
4. Três Palavras (Osvaldo Farrés, Adapt. Clóvis Mello)
5. Drão (Gilberto Gil)
6. Não Tenho Medo da Morte (Gilberto Gil)
7. Expresso 2222 (Gilberto Gil)
8. Toda Menina Baiana (Gilberto Gil)
9. São João Xangô Menino (Caetano Veloso, Gilberto Gil)
10. Nossa Gente (Avisa Lá) (Roque Carvalho)
11. Andar Com Fé (Gilberto Gil)
12. Filhos de Gandhi (Gilberto Gil)
13. Desde Que O Samba É Samba (Caetano Veloso)
14. Domingo No Parque (Gilberto Gil)
15. A Luz de Tieta (Caetano Veloso)

2017
ANOS 70 AO VIVO (BACK IN BAHIA)

Label: Discobertas — DBOX65
Live from Rio de Janeiro,
May 12, 1972

1. Back In Bahia (Gilberto Gil)
2. O Sonho Acabou (Gilberto Gil)
3. Expresso 2222 (Gilberto Gil)
4. O Canto da Ema (Alventino Cavalcanti, Aires Viana, João do Vale)
5. Aquele Abraço (Gilberto Gil)
6. Sai do Sereno (Onildo Almeida)
7. O Bom Jogador (Gilberto Gil)
8. Madalena (Entra Em Beco, Sai Em Beco) (Isidoro, Adpt. Gilberto Gil)
9. Cultura E Civilização (Gilberto Gil)
10. Brand New Dream (Gilberto Gil)
11. Oriente (Gilberto Gil)
12. Chiclete Com Banana (Gordurinha, Almira Castilho)
13. Back In Bahia (Gilberto Gil); Atrás do Trio Elétrico (Caetano Veloso)

2017
**ANOS 70 AO VIVO
(UMEBOSHI)**

Label: Discobertas — DBOX65
Live from Rio de Janeiro,
April 1973

1. Essa É Pra Tocar no Rádio (Gilberto Gil)
2. Iansã (Gilberto Gil, Caetano Veloso)
3. Doente, Morena (Duda Machado, Gilberto Gil)
4. Duplo Sentido (Gilberto Gil)
5. Cidade Do Salvador (Gilberto Gil)
6. Imbalança (Luiz Gonzaga, Zé Dantas)
7. Ladeira da Preguiça (Gilberto Gil)
8. Umeboshi (Gilberto Gil)
9. Minha Nega na Janela (Germano Mathias, Doca)
10. Tradição (Gilberto Gil)
11. Preciso Aprender A Só Ser (Gilberto Gil)
12. Meio de Campo (Gilberto Gil)
13. Eu Só Quero Um Xodó (Dominguinhos, Anastácia)
14. Edyth Cooper (Gilberto Gil); Back In Bahia (Gilberto Gil); Procissão (Gilberto Gil)
15. Preciso Aprender A Só Ser (Gilberto Gil)
16. Iansã (Gilberto Gil, Caetano Veloso)
17. Cidade de Salvador (Gilberto Gil)

2017
ANOS 70 AO VIVO
(AO VIVO NA USP
DISC 1)

Label: Discobertas — DBOX65
Live from USP, São Paulo,
May 1973

1. Oriente (Gilberto Gil)
2. Apresentação (Gilberto Gil)
3. Chiclete Com Banana (Gordurinha/Almira Castilho)
4. Minha Nega na Janela (Germano Mathias, Doca)
5. Senhor Delegado (Antoninho Lopes, Jaú)
6. Eu Quero Um Samba (Haroldo Barbosa, Janet de Almeida)
7. Meio de Campo (Gilberto Gil)
8. Cálice (Chico Buarque, Gilberto Gil)
9. O Sonho Acabou (Gilberto Gil)
10. Ladeira da Preguiça (Gilberto Gil)
11. Expresso 2222 (Gilberto Gil)
12. Procissão (Gilberto Gil)
13. Domingo No Parque (Gilberto Gil)
14. Umeboshi (Gilberto Gil)

2017
**ANOS 70 AO VIVO
(AO VIVO NA USP
DISC 2)**

Label: Discobertas — DBOX65
Live from USP, São Paulo,
May 1973

1. Objeto Sim, Objeto Não (Gilberto Gil)
2. Ele e Eu (Gilberto Gil)
3. Duplo Sentido (Gilberto Gil)
4. Cidade Do Salvador (Gilberto Gil)
5. Iansã (Gilberto Gil, Caetano Veloso)
6. Eu Só Quero Um Xodó (Dominguinhos, Anastácia)
7. Edyth Cooper (Gilberto Gil)
8. Back In Bahia (Gilberto Gil)
9. Afoxé (Dorival Caymmi); Oração de Mãe Menininha (Dorival Caymmi)
10. Preciso Aprender A Só Ser (Gilberto Gil)
11. Cálice (Chico Buarque, Gilberto Gil)

2017
TRINCA DE ASES
GAL COSTA, GILBERTO GIL
E NANDO REIS

Label: Biscoito Fino — BF 532-4
Live from Multishow TV Channel

1. Trinca De Ases (Gilberto Gil); Dupla De Ás (Nando Reis)
2. Palco (Gilberto Gil); Baby (Caetano Veloso)
3. All Star (Nando Reis)
4. Espatódea (Nando Reis); O Seu Lado De Cá (Nando Reis)
5. Esotérico (Gilberto Gil)
6. Cores Vivas (Gilberto Gil); Água-Viva (Nando Reis)
7. Retiros Espirituais (Gilberto Gil); Copo Vazio (Gilberto Gil)
8. Meu Amigo, Meu Herói (Gilberto Gil)
9. Relicário (Nando Reis); Pérola Negra (Luiz Melodia)
10. Refavela (Gilberto Gil)
11. Ela (Gilberto Gil)
12. Tocarte (Gilberto Gil, Nando Reis)
13. Dois Rios (Samuel Rosa, Lô Borges, Nando Reis)
14. Lately (Stevie Wonder) Nada Mais (Lately) (Stevie Wonder,
Adapt. Ronaldo Bastos)
15. Por Onde Andei (Nando Reis)
16. Nos Barracos da Cidade (Gilberto Gil, Liminha)
17. O Segundo Sol (Nando Reis)
18. A Gente Precisa Ver O Luar (Gilberto Gil); Barato Total (Gilberto Gil)

2018
OK OK OK

Label: Biscoito Fino — BF 574-2
Producers: Bem Gil and Liminha

1. Ok Ok Ok (Gilberto Gil)
2. Na Real (Gilberto Gil)
3. Sereno (Gilberto Gil, Bem Gil)
4. Uma Coisa Bonitinha (Gilberto Gil, João Donato) Featuring: João Donato
5. Quatro Pedacinhos (Gilberto Gil)
6. Ouço (Gilberto Gil)
7. Lia E Deia (Gilberto Gil)
8. Jacintho (Gilberto Gil)
9. Yamandu (Gilberto Gil) Featuring: Yamandú Costa
10. Tartaruguê (Gilberto Gil) Featuring: João Donato
11. Sol De Maria (Gilberto Gil)
12. Prece (Gilberto Gil)
13. Afogamento (Gilberto Gil, Jorge Bastos Moreno)
Featuring: Roberta Sá
14. Kalil (Gilberto Gil)
15. Pela Internet 2 (Gilberto Gil)

2019
GIL
TRILHA SONORA DO
ESPETÁCULO DO
GRUPO CORPO

Label: Gegê Produções
Producer: Bem Gil

1. Intro (Gilberto Gil)
2. Choro Nº 1 (Gilberto Gil)
3. Improviso Choro Nº 1 (Gilberto Gil)
4. Intro (Gilberto Gil)
5. Seraphimu (Gilberto Gil)
6. Improviso Seraphimu (Gilberto Gil)
7. Solo Balafon (Gilberto Gil)
8. Intro (Gilberto Gil)
9. Fragmento Lírico (Gilberto Gil)
10. Improviso Fragmento Lírico (Gilberto Gil)
11. Circulo (Gilberto Gil)
12. Triangulo (Gilberto Gil)
13. Quadrado (Gilberto Gil)
14. Retângulo (Gilberto Gil)
15. Pentágono (Gilberto Gil)
16. Gil (Gilberto Gil)

2020
GIL E BAIANASYSTEM
AO VIVO EM SALVADOR

Label: Noize — NRC036
Producer: Russo Passapusso

SIDE A
1. Is This Love (Bob Marley)
2. Nos Barracos Da Cidade (Gilberto Gil, Liminha); Systema Fobica
(BaianaSystem)
3. Extra (Gilberto Gil)

SIDE B
1. Pessoa Nefasta (Gilberto Gil)

2. Sarará Miolo (Gilberto Gil)

3. Emoriô (Gilberto Gil, João Donato); Dia Da Caça (Russo Passapusso)

4. Água (Antonio Carlos E Jocafi, Roberto Barreto, Russo Passapusso,
Ubiratan Marques)

2021
SÃO JOÃO AO VIVO EM ARARAS

Label: Gegê Produções

1. Fé Na Festa (Gilberto Gil)
2. Dança da Moda (Luiz Gonzaga, Zé Dantas)
3. Óia Eu Aqui de Novo (Antônio Barros)
4. Assim, Sim (Gilberto Gil)
5. Respeita Januário (Luiz Gonzaga, Humberto Teixeira)
6. O Xote das Meninas (Luiz Gonzaga, Zé Dantas)
7. Conversa Gil e Preta Gil (Gilberto Gil)
8. Eu Só Quero Um Xodó (Dominguinhos, Anastácia) Featuring: Preta Gil
9. Asa Branca (Luiz Gonzaga, Humberto Teixeira)
10. A Volta da Asa Branca (Luiz Gonzaga, Zé Dantas)
11. São João Xangô Menino (Caetano Veloso, Gilberto Gil)
12. Esperando Na Janela (Targino Gondim, Manuca Almeida, Raimundinho do Acordeon)
13. Qui Nem Jiló (Luiz Gonzaga, Humberto Teixeira)
14. Pedras Que Cantam (Dominguinhos, Fausto Nilo)
15. Conversa Gil e Mestrinho (Gilberto Gil)
16. Isso Aqui Tá Bom Demais (Dominguinhos, Nando Cordel)
17. Toda Menina Baiana (Gilberto Gil)
18. Olha Pro Céu (Luiz Gonzaga, José Fernandes)

2022
EM CASA COM OS GIL

Label: Gegê Produções

1. Palco (Gilberto Gil)
2. Barato Total (Gilberto Gil)
3. Back In Bahia (Gilberto Gil)
4. Esotérico (Gilberto Gil)
5. Queremos Saber (Gilberto Gil)
Featuring: Fran, Ana Cláudia Lomelino (Mãeana)
6. Super-Homem (A Canção) (Gilberto Gil)
7. Drão (Gilberto Gil) Featuring: Preta Gil
8. Sereno (Gilberto Gil, Bem Gil)
9. Não Tenho Medo da Morte (Gilberto Gil)
10. Cores Vivas (Gilberto Gil)
11. Babá Alapalá (Gilberto Gil)
12. Touche Pas a Mon Pote (Gilberto Gil)
13. Feliz Por Um Triz (Gilberto Gil)
14. Sítio do Pica-Pau Amarelo (Gilberto Gil)
Featuring: Preta Gil, Fran, Flor Gil
15. Realce (Gilberto Gil)

www.ingramcontent.com/pod-product-compliance
Lightning Source LLC
LaVergne TN
LVHW072224150726

843469LV00057B/2314